A Director's Guide to Corporate Financial Reporting

A Director's Guide to Corporate Financial Reporting

Krista Fiolleau, Kris Hoang, and Karim Jamal

University of Alberta

First published in 2010 by
Business Expert Press, LLC
222 East 46th Street, New York, NY 10017
www.businessexpertpress.com

ISBN-13: 978-1-60649-131-7 (paperback)
ISBN-10: 1-60649-131-7 (paperback)

ISBN-13: 978-1-60649-132-4 (e-book)
ISBN-10: 1-60649-132-4 (e-book)

DOI 10.4128/9781606491317

A publication in the Business Expert Press Corporate Governance collection

Collection ISSN: 1948-0407 (print)
Collection ISSN: 1948-0415 (electronic)

Cover design by Jonathan Pennell
Interior design by Scribe, Inc.

First edition: February 2010

10 9 8 7 6 5 4 3 2 1

Printed in the United States of America.

Abstract

This book is designed for current and prospective corporate directors, as well as executives in business courses who want to gain a better understanding of accounting in a board setting. Corporate directors and managers are under pressure from constant changes in the law (especially the Sarbanes-Oxley Act of 2002 and a move toward International Financial Reporting Standards) and demands by shareholders and the public to be more informed, vigilant, and involved in the governance of business organizations. One area in particular, accounting and financial reporting, has been a source of great consternation for directors. Breakdowns in internal control, reporting scandals, restatements, and outright accounting fraud have made accounting a source of dread and confusion for corporate directors. We have designed a guidebook with action steps, probing questions, and cases to help directors address key accounting issues that boards face. We discuss what accounting tries to accomplish, how well it achieves its purpose, and why and how accounting and financial reporting go awry. Emphasizing that accounting is a nonneutral financial reporting process, we show directors that accounting is a process by which financial information is recorded, classified, summarized, interpreted, and communicated. By focusing on key issues, including fair value reporting, performance measurement, and the board's role in policy formation, directors can learn to effectively scrutinize and advise their organizations about accounting practices and understand the impact of accounting issues on the operation of their organization.

Keywords

Accounting, corporate governance, internal control, fraud, restatements

Contents

Introduction

Corporate governance consists of a set of structures, policies, processes, and people that help administer and control business organizations. The key agents tasked with promoting an effective system of corporate governance are the board and the directors who serve on them. Corporate directors are under tremendous pressure from regulations (especially the Sarbanes-Oxley Act of 2002 and the International Financial Reporting Standards [IFRS] convergence) and demands from shareholders and the public who want to be more informed, vigilant, and involved in the governance of business organizations. One area in particular, namely, accounting and financial reporting, has been a source of great consternation for directors. Breakdowns in internal control, reporting scandals, restatements, and outright accounting fraud have made accounting a source of dread and confusion for corporate directors.

Public discussions about accounting involve frequent use of slogans such as "truth," "neutrality," "transparency," and "consistency." While these are appealing slogans, they obscure rather than elucidate the role that accounting plays in directing an organization and the reasons why modern business organizations have failed to achieve such ideals. Our goal in this book is to get past these slogans, which we consider to be largely erroneous and misleading. We discuss what accounting tries to do, how well it achieves its purpose, and why and how accounting and financial reporting go awry. Current and prospective corporate directors, as well as executives in business courses who want to gain a better understanding of accounting in a board setting, can use this understanding to move discussions beyond financial reports. By examining the accounting issues and examples presented in this book, directors will be able to identify and articulate the impact of accounting matters on broader organizational issues to navigate their boards through this time of transition. Several segments also include forward-thinking approaches that directors can consider in order to steer their boards and organizations to the forefront of the accounting transition.

It is a popular notion that accounting is a reporting system that simply reports the truth. Accounting is often viewed as an objective scorekeeping system like those used in a variety of sports. Managers like to say that they play the game, and accounting simply reports the score or performance of the organization. This notion of truth in accounting creates demands for transparency, neutrality, and consistency. However, this notion of truth is misleading and not achievable by real organizations. Business organizations have a complex set of assets and liabilities, the value of which will be realized in the future. Since we need a financial report today about claims that will be realized in the future, accounting can provide an approximate representation based on a series of estimates and judgments rather than on hard facts or truth. This means that accounting is a technology that creates an "accounting representation" of the financial condition of a business organization but not a true representation. Like all representations and models, accounting will represent some features of organizations well, some in an acceptable way, some poorly, and leave some out or obscure other important features. Given the information demands and inherent limitation of accounting technology, the first objective of this book is to help directors understand what accounting does well, badly, and not at all.

In the past, accounting was based on actual transactions and was historical in nature, as it focused on providing information for assessing accountability of various corporate agents. In recent years, accounting standard setters have been attempting to make accounting more future oriented to help investors predict future cash flows. This shift toward "fair value reporting" in accounting practices is increasing the use of market prices, outputs of complex quantitative models, and human judgment. Accounting is becoming more complex, subjective, and further removed from any objective notion of truthful representations. As managers are gaining more discretion over accounting practices, the second objective of this book is to help directors understand the role of accounting policy choices and accounting estimates in creating a better (or worse) representation of the financial condition of an organization.

The book is organized as follows:

Chapters 1 and 2 provide a broad overview and description of the process by which financial information is recorded. There is a special emphasis on the importance of internal control as a key function of the accounting system.

Chapters 3 through 6 provide a description of the process by which financial information is classified, summarized (i.e., aggregated), interpreted, and communicated to users of financial statements. Accounting creates a highly aggregated report, and a new perspective on transparency must be applied to understand the representation reported in the financial statements. In these chapters, we discuss the claim that financial statements have become very complex, and most users cannot understand what is being reported. We question the meaning of transparency if users cannot understand an organization's financial condition.

Chapters 7 and 8 discuss why restatements occur and the special cases of private companies and not-for-profit organizations. Accounting has historically insisted on a "one-size-fits-all" set of rules. However, there is a growing realization that complex accounting rules developed for use by very large and complex public companies are costly and increasingly inappropriate for private companies and not-for-profit organizations. A process is underway to create different sets of accounting rules for different types of organizations. Accounting is undeniably in a state of transition.

Each chapter in the book has a summary of key issues that directors should consider and a set of recommendations for actions that directors can take. We use Safeway Inc.,[1] one of North America's largest food and drug retailers, as an illustrative example of accounting issues and disclosures throughout the book. Safeway Inc. operates retail stores and manufacturing and processing plants in the United States and western Canada. Safeway's financial statements reflect a moderate level of accounting complexity. Through the discussion of accounting issues and use of illustrative examples in this book, our objective is to help directors to be better informed about accounting and financial reporting and to better discharge their duty to improve governance of the business organizations and shareholders they serve.

CHAPTER 1

Reporting the Truth

A Quest for Neutrality and Transparency

First umpire: "Some are balls and some are strikes, and I call 'em as they are."
Second umpire: "Some are balls and some are strikes, and I call 'em as I see 'em."
Third umpire: "Some are balls and some are strikes, but they ain't nothin' 'til I call 'em."

—Three views of baseball umpires

Accounting as a Process for Business Reporting

The Oxford Dictionary defines accounting as "the process of or skill in keeping and verifying accounts." Accounting is more comprehensively understood as a process for business reporting by which financial information about a business is recorded, classified, summarized, interpreted and communicated. Most people think of accounting as a mechanical scoring process that reports the true financial condition of an organization. Accounting has existed as a business reporting process for several centuries, yet it is widely misunderstood. The business press focuses only on accounting scandals (fraud and restatements) and the U.S. Securities and Exchange Commission and regulators require that financial statements record all assets and liabilities on the balance sheet. Senior corporate officers are being asked to sign certifications stating that the financial statements represent the "true" financial condition of the company. Accounting is portrayed as a neutral reporting system like the rules of a sports game. Any misuse of accounting is attributed to "evil" managers who are trying to exploit shareholders and other participants. Accounting is thought to be like the first umpire, who "calls them as they are."

This view of accounting is incomplete. Accounting has never reported all the assets and liabilities of a corporation. Accounting has also never reported the true financial condition of the company. What accounting creates is an *accounting representation* of the financial condition of the company. Accounting highlights and reports a variety of assets and liabilities in a manner determined by the measurement technology of accounting. A company that is a going concern has a mix of tangible and intangible assets and liabilities, the realization of which will only be known in the future. The need for periodic (e.g., annual) reporting means that accounting must create a financial representation of the economic condition of a company. This representation is not the concrete truth. It is an abstraction or an estimate of what is likely to occur in the future. Accounting measures some assets and liabilities well (e.g., cash), measures some mechanically (e.g., depreciation of buildings), measures some badly (e.g., goodwill, stock option expense, leases), and doesn't measure some at all (e.g., research and development [R&D],[1] a company's reputation in the community, various environmental liabilities that are in the distant future).

Many CEOs and CFOs have reservations about certifying that their financial statements represent the true financial condition of the company. Moreover, auditors usually require that their opinions be offered "in accordance with Generally Accepted Accounting Principles" (GAAP). Their fondness for GAAP is not just to eliminate legal ambiguity; the auditor also understands that the financial statements report an accounting representation, and not a true representation, of the financial condition of a company.

The rhetoric of accounting standard setters and securities regulators is about achieving neutrality and transparency—as opposed to excessive conservatism or optimism—in accounting reports. The neutrality of actual accounting numbers is debatable. Historically, accounting standards have favored the interests of banks and owners of companies, producing conservatively biased historical cost financial statements. These accounting standards were developed from a notion of accountability, whereby accounting helps an agent to report how assets were used and acquired during an annual reporting period. Since the 1970s, the Financial Accounting Standards Board (FASB in the United States, AcSB in Canada, and IASB internationally) moved toward favoring the interests of financial analysts and management and the production of fair value oriented financial statements. The result is a shift in focus from an accountability orientation toward a future decision-making orientation, where accounting assists investors in predicting the future cash flows of a company.

This move toward fair value has introduced tremendous complexity into accounting. Many people with a good understanding of business are unable to understand the accounting numbers and disclosures provided in financial statements. Fair value reporting has the potential, however, to make the balance sheet better represent the true economic condition of some assets and liabilities of the company. At the same time, fair value reporting impairs the usefulness of the income statement and distorts the representation of some other assets and liabilities.

An interesting question is whether transparency is achieved when only a few specialized and highly expert readers, particularly industry competitors and financial analysts, can understand a great deal about a company, but most other people cannot. Certainly, it is a misnomer to call accounting standards "Generally Accepted." Most accountants have no say in the determination of accounting standards. As accounting standard setting becomes more concentrated and geographically distant with an International Accounting Standards Board (IASB) developing global standards in London, accountants in other regions will have less (or no) influence in the process. Many professional accountants, auditors, and even board members find it difficult to understand financial statements. Since accounting is less "generally understood," it has the potential for destabilizing markets and creating bubbles and extreme deviations from equilibrium behavior; that is, clever investors can profit at the expense of less sophisticated investors. While securities regulators are supposed to protect the small investor, the accounting standards boards respond mostly to pressure from highly sophisticated investors who demand very complex information. The accounting standards boards are heading down a path that could make financial statements completely incomprehensible to the small investor.

The Migration of Accounting to Fair Value Reporting

Historical cost accounting is the origin of our accounting system. The system was primarily put in place to ensure that there was a proper accounting of the money that was collected by an organization and the resources that flowed out of the organization. This led to a system that was based on three key features:

1. *Realization.* As accounting was primarily a tracking system for resources, all transactions were booked in the financial statements when they occurred. The key determinant of the timing of the recording of a transaction was when the transaction actually took place. The resulting accounting system was structured around the realization of transactions.

2. *Income statement recognition.* All transactions were recorded in the income statement when they occurred. This technique provided an immediate tracking of the transactional flow of resources through the income statement.

3. *Hard and verifiable numbers.* Since all entries made in the financial statements were based on transactions entered into in the current period, these numbers were both verifiable and concrete. There was little or no estimation required on the balance sheet, and all transactions were presented on the income statement for the period.

In the current financial statement environment, stakeholders are continually requesting forward-looking financial information from the financial statements. In response, standards have moved away from a historical cost transactional structure toward a forward-looking current value structure. Where does this move in standards leave us in relation to the three key features listed above?

1. *Realization.* In the current environment of fair value accounting, we have lost the transactional structure of the old system. Financial statement items are adjusted, and items are recorded commensurate with the passage of time rather than at the time a transaction is executed. Managers book unrealized gains and losses, leaving accounting reports vulnerable to wishful thinking and illusory gains.

2. *Income statement recognition.* Due to a requirement to adjust items to market value at period end, the income statement can become quite volatile. To constrain this volatility, it is important to allow some items to bypass the income statement. This bypass is achieved by the introduction of a concept called "other comprehensive income." Certain financial items can now bypass the income statement and simply result in an adjustment of equity through the statement of comprehensive income. The absence of these charges in the income statement hinders the ability of accounting rules to discipline management for all costs incurred by the organization.

3. *Hard and verifiable numbers.* Are all numbers hard, verifiable, and auditable now? The lack of transaction-based entries and the widespread use of estimates have increased volatility in the financial statements. Especially in a crumbling economy, where asset values are declining, it is less likely that even valuation specialists will arrive at a consensus on fair values. Items on the financial statements can no longer be easily traced back to an economic transaction and are now in the "grey zone" for auditing. Management has much more leeway in influencing the financial statements and may or may not choose to take on the cost of hiring a valuation specialist.

We are now faced with asking *what will be the new disciplinary measure in this fair value world?*

Boards should recognize that fair value accounting gives them the opportunity to illuminate items that were previously hidden from users of the financial statements (e.g., loss in value of financial instruments held by a company). With more detailed disclosure and visibility of certain items through fair value accounting, we can increase understanding of the future prospects of the company. As to the extensive use of estimates within fair value accounting, a record could be kept of managers' and companies' accuracy in estimation that could be used by the board and the capital markets as a signal of the reliability of the estimations and the manager's ability. Issues around management estimation will be discussed in chapter 5 on interpretation. Finally, accounting standards boards may benefit from the selective use of fair value reporting in areas where it is potentially most useful, rather than using it throughout the financial statements.

Implementation

Accounting suffers from a problem with implementation. Financial statements are prepared by management. Management, however, is not a neutral umpire implementing accounting standards according to a textbook. Managers have self-interest in the numbers reported in the financial statements. Even if accounting standard setters could achieve the goal of writing neutral accounting standards, management could distort the application of the accounting standards. The best possible situation is one in which accounting standards are neutral, but accounting numbers include some bias.[2] The degree of bias in accounting numbers would depend on a variety of environmental factors, such as the legal regime, the quality of auditing, the monitoring by the board (audit committee), and the strictness of securities law enforcement. For example, countries with weak enforcement by securities commissions and limited legal liability, such as Canada, suggest potential for more biased financial statements versus those in countries with highly litigious environments, such as the United States.

Management Compensation

Executive compensation packages largely contribute to the implementation problem of accounting. Management acts as an agent of shareholders who are looking to earn a profit on their investment in the organization. The stewardship role of accounting allows shareholders to evaluate management as a steward of their investments. An agency problem exists when management pursues its own interests rather than those of the shareholders. For example, a manager may know that he is leaving the organization by the end of the year and push sales to customers before he leaves so that he can maximize his sales-based bonus; however, this sales push results in lower sales in the following year and can reduce the value of the organization. Compensation contracts should, therefore, be structured to align the behaviors of management with the long-term interests of shareholders. That is, compensation should induce managers to make decisions consistent with the organization's mandate to undertake positive net present value (NPV) projects and reject negative NPV projects. In addition to salary, the compensation package may include performance-based bonuses, share ownership, and stock options as tools to provide incentives to managers to make decisions that maximize shareholder value. However, boards must be cognizant that these elements of the compensation package are either directly or indirectly tied to accounting numbers, which could induce managers to make undesirable decisions in financial reporting, such as earnings manipulation. Furthermore, linking performance-based pay to any accounting number (and even many nonaccounting based metrics such as stock options) can distort managers' behavior in order to achieve favorable accounting results by rejecting positive NPV projects and selecting negative NPV projects, thereby influencing operations to achieve an accounting result.

Compensation contracts are a direct function of accounting numbers when they involve bonuses based on financial targets, particularly earnings and revenue. In order to maximize bonuses and achieve these financial targets, managers might wish to increase or decrease earnings, giving the impression of a smooth, steady increase in earnings over time,[3] or falsely attribute negative financial results to one-time events (conversely, they may attribute positive results from one-time events to more persistent, substantive operating activities). The following are a few of the many ways in which managers may manipulate accounting earnings:

- *Big bath*: an income-decreasing accounting procedure undertaken in periods with poor performance, where the manager takes a considerable loss all in one period, such as writing down the value of assets, so that performance in subsequent years appears better.
- *Cookie jar reserves*: an income-decreasing accounting choice made in periods with strong performance, where the manager is overly conservative in estimating provisions, such as the likelihood of collecting accounts receivable, so that in future periods the estimate can be revised upward and amounts brought back into income when performance falls short of targets.
- *Revenue recognition*: a choice to shift recognition of revenue into different periods as management is required to meet targets or smooth spikes in earnings, either by recognizing revenue prematurely or by recognizing revenue that is not

substantiated by actual transactions (such as shipping excess
goods to customers beyond what has been ordered).

- *Classification of transitory items*: the use of the "extraordinary"
  or "unusual items" label to suggest that losses are nonrecur-
  ring and will not be present in future periods. The manager
  may also give the impression that transitory (one-time) gains
  will persist in future periods and are attributable to ongoing,
  successful operation of the organization. One of the problems
  with fair value accounting is that it lumps together persistent,
  real cash flows with transitory, unrealized values that are volatile and change as management revises its estimates.[4]

When performance-based bonuses form part of the compensation contract, boards will observe a floor-and-ceiling effect in earnings. The
presence of bonuses induces management to use the methods above or
other means to manipulate income downward when the level of earnings
will not result in any incremental bonus. Likewise, managers will make
earnings-increasing accounting decisions when actual performance falls
just below the threshold for bonuses. If results are considerably below the
level required to achieve the bonus, managers may attempt to severely
reduce earnings so that their performance appears better in future periods. Bonuses that are based on earnings growth each year induce managers to manipulate earnings so that they steadily increase year after year
rather than increasing and decreasing erratically and meeting targets in
one year and failing in another. Clearly, contracts involving bonuses that
are meant to induce managers to maximize firm value can lead to undesirable financial accounting choices.

Compensation may also indirectly depend on accounting numbers
when they incorporate share ownership or stock options. Share and
option value are influenced by reported accounting numbers, such as
revenue or earnings, that are subject to the aforementioned accounting manipulations. Of more concern is the unlimited upside potential
and absence of risk of loss for managers who receive stock option compensation. These conditions pave the way for earnings management of
greater magnitude—potential payoff for managers is very high if the market accepts the accounting manipulation, and managers risk no loss if

the accounting manipulation reduces firm value. Such incentive schemes encourage extreme risk-taking behavior and create circumstances that can lead to huge frauds, such as the Enron scandal. The probability and magnitude of accounting manipulation depends largely on the pressure that incentive compensation places on managers. Boards must, therefore, be cautious in their use of performance-based compensation and be aware that the use of incentives also creates pressure for accounting earnings management.

The External Auditor

At best, the external auditor can only provide a very limited constraint on management's self-serving reporting.[5] The limited effectiveness of external auditors is not well understood. The nature of actual accounting practice is one where the accounting standards are published, but transactions are done by managers who know the accounting standards. A manager intent on achieving a particular reporting objective can often structure a transaction to obtain the intended result. It is very difficult for an auditor to restrain a manager who has structured a transaction to obtain a particular accounting treatment. Under historical cost accounting, it was at least plausible to argue that the auditor was acting like the second umpire in the quote at the start of this chapter: "I call 'em as I see 'em." The switch toward fair value accounting makes that claim less plausible. Fair value accounting gives management more discretion in determining numbers reported in financial statements. Accounting is now becoming like the third umpire—"they ain't nothin' 'til I call 'em"— except the umpire is management, principally the CEO and CFO. Under fair value accounting, management reports "from the view of management." The external auditor can place some bounds on management's self-serving judgments but is much less effective at restraining management than under the previous historical cost accounting system. Whether the increased complexity, the increased exposure to managerial fraud, and the increased self-serving judgment are worth it is the subject of current accounting debate. It is important to note, as this debate continues, that the lack of effective legal sanctions and the ineffective securities regulation enforcement in certain jurisdictions will be more problematic as we move toward fair value–oriented accounting policies.

The issuance of new independence rules has also changed the relationship with the external auditor. This new ruling requires that the auditor be independent throughout the audit and engagement period. In the past, the auditor was often seen by management as a source of expert opinion and information in regard to a client's accounting policies and issues. With the dawn of this new era, the auditor is no longer free to be the open advisor of management and is instead restricted in its role. This means that management must make judgments aided by the audit committee and possibly by external consultants who have been hired to assist the company, yet management faces the possibility of having a dispute with the auditor at year-end. The new reality is costly and can create a strained relationship with the external auditor.

The irony is that despite all the Sarbanes-Oxley Act (SOX) reforms, the potential for managerial fraud and self-serving financial reporting is actually increasing, and we continue to observe corporate scandals and economic breakdowns. The effectiveness of external auditors in restraining management is being impaired. The accounting standards boards are taking a gamble that "fair value" reporting will increase the relevance of financial statements and will not lead to more fraud and distorted financial reporting. Whether this is the right gamble will be known over time, though the potential for more financial reporting disasters is high.

The Board's Role: Working With the External Auditor

The external auditor is an integral part of the overall quality of the financial statements. Since all publicly traded companies and the majority of not-for-profit enterprises require an audit, this section is intended to provide an overall understanding of the role of the auditor in an organization's financial reporting and also provide a brief process description of the various roles the auditor can take for the board and management.

It is important to understand that the financial statements, note disclosure, and annual report are ultimately the responsibility of management. In essence, legally management owns these reports. The auditor can provide advice and guidance to management, but the final decision as to the accounting policies, content, and presentation of the financial statements is the responsibility of management and the board. What is the auditor responsible for? The auditor is solely responsible for the auditor's report. It is the provision of this report and the opinion that it provides that allows the auditor to influence what management presents within the financial statements. Although the auditor investigates the activities and balances within the financial statements to determine if they are materially misstated with reference to the reporting criteria, when a material misstatement is discovered, it is up to management to decide how and whether to correct it. It is important for the board to understand that the final presentation within the financial statements is the responsibility of management and that the auditor is only responsible for conducting tests and rendering opinions in the auditor's report.

It is imperative that the board has a clear understanding of the responsibility of the auditor. An expectations gap arises when there is conflict between statement users and the auditors due to different expectations. Auditors are required to conduct their examination of the financial statement to meet the requirement of their professional standards (Canadian or U.S. Generally Accepted Auditing Standards or International Auditing Standards). Many users believe auditors guarantee the accuracy of the financial statements, and some even believe that the auditor is guaranteeing the financial viability of the company. The board of directors cannot rely on the auditor to prevent management from making poor financial or business decisions or even to highlight these decisions to the board. The auditors will present any major disagreements that arise between management and themselves during the course of the audit, particularly about financial reporting, but they are not directly responsible for evaluating management's operating, financing, and investing decisions.

Auditors act as a moderate constraint on management behavior. They can stop management from deviating from GAAP in a material way by threatening to provide a negative auditor's report, but they have no mechanism to push management to provide better disclosure. In essence, the auditor is available to ensure that management complies with accounting rules (and thus enforces a minimum standard of reporting) but is not able to force management to adopt best practices. Due to independence concerns, the auditor may be reluctant to provide much advice to even lead management in this direction. The major challenge is that auditors in the current litigious environment are concerned with public perception of the auditor's independence (i.e., their objectivity and freedom from bias and leniency with management). It is thus important for the board to ask appropriate questions of the auditor and management to determine where they sit in the realm of best practices. This suggestion is discussed in detail in chapter 3 on policy formation and chapter 6 on corporate disclosure.

Another challenge to the board is that outside users of the financial statements have difficulty in evaluating audit quality. Users can observe that the auditor issued a clean (unqualified) opinion but cannot tell whether the audit was thorough, insightful, efficient, or reflective of some other dimension of quality. In other words, users have difficulty judging whether an auditor did a good job. However, other characteristics of the auditor or audit firm are publicly visible as approximate, though incomplete, indicators of how committed the organization is to getting a high-quality audit from a credible auditor. Examples of such traits of the auditor and audit firm that might serve as indicators include: firm size (especially Big 4 vs. non-Big 4 auditors), industry-specific expertise, established market leadership in the local geographic region, strong relationships with regulators, and access to specialty resources (e.g., publications, databases, and workshops). These traits should be well matched to the organization's needs and fit into the public perception of the scope of the organization's audit. An example of an audit firm inappropriately matched with an organization's scope is the three-person firm Friehling & Horowitz, auditors of Bernie Madoff's multibillion-dollar fund, which is notorious as one of the largest financial scandals in recent history.[6] Organizations with this scope of operation typically appoint one of the largest global audit firms as their service providers because both insiders and outsiders instantly recognize the brands of these firms and the level of quality that they represent.

Beyond rendering audit opinions and acting as a constraint on management, the auditor may also play a more process-oriented role. The board and management must decide what "type" of auditor is the most beneficial to the organization's management style. From a process standpoint, there are various ways in which the auditor can interact with management and the board, particularly when it comes to the discussion of major accounting issues. The auditor's approach to issues is partly determined by management's approach, but an auditor also has his or her own individual style, which is illustrated by looking at the following three approaches to the discussion of a new accounting issue with the client. If we assume that management has been forthcoming with regards to the issue (which is not always the case), then the auditor can address this issue in the following ways:

1. The auditor can indicate to management that they would like management to investigate the issue on their own and develop their own opinion and solution prior to the auditor discussing it further.
2. The auditor can provide management with reference material and industry information in regard to the issue and then have management develop their own opinion and solution.
3. The auditor can provide their opinion as to the appropriate solution with reference material to back it up and then have management decide whether they agree or not.

The quality of the auditor is not necessarily different in these three approaches; it is simply a difference in process orientation. It is also critical that the board and management understand which process their auditor is currently following. Should the auditor's approach fall short of the organization's expectations, the board might consider having the auditor change its process to align with the directors and/or management's preferences. Review the following case in the context of a revenue recognition issue for an illustration of these process differences, paying particular attention to the different styles of the auditor.

Illustrative Case: Auditor Types

ConGroup (CG) is a publicly traded construction company with annual billings of $2 billion per year. Over the last 5 years, CG's average income before taxes was $40 million dollars. The company has $200 million in working capital, $300 million in shareholders' equity, and total assets of $400 million. CG uses the percentage-of-completion method (based on total subcontractor costs incurred to date) to account for construction contracts.

CG has been developing relationships with major hydro companies across Canada in order to enter a new line of business. Early in its current fiscal year, CG was awarded a $1.6 billion-dollar construction management contract to build a power plant in northern Manitoba. This contract is substantially larger than previous contracts and is qualitatively different from previous contracts. This type of contract will require some adjustment to the cost forecast and budget model used by CG, as well as much on-the-job learning by all members of the company. In the short term, there is more uncertainty about the accuracy of the costs forecast for this type of contract. Management is delighted to have won this contract and expects that success on this contract will enable CG to win more large dollar value contracts across the country and even internationally. Management can foresee the need to go back to the capital markets to raise additional capital reasonably soon to finance large projects of this magnitude. Management is thus keen to show success on this project, both to the board of directors and to potential investors. Hence, management wants to reconsider its revenue recognition policy. Contract details are as follows:

1. The scheduled contract duration is 36 months.
2. Construction management fee is $86,400,000.
3. The construction management fee includes direct personnel (construction manager, scheduler, estimator, project accountants, superintendents, safety managers, and other administrative personnel); equipment rent; general operating expenses of the site office; overhead of any kind; contractor profit; insurance; bonding; and financing costs.
4. All subcontracts are between CG and the subcontractor. CG is totally responsible for the performance of their subcontractors.

CG's budget for this project is as follows:

Subcontract costs		$1,513,600,000
Management costs		$86,400,000
Consisting of:		
Equipment costs	13,000,000	
Labor costs [720,000 hours]	36,000,000	
Living-out allowances	3,000,000	
Site office expenses	1,000,000	
Profit	33,400,000	
		$1,600,000,000

At year-end, the contract has been in progress for 10 months. CG has billed the owner $338,000,000 to date. This billing is made up of $314,000,000 of subcontractor expenses and $24,000,000 for the construction management fee. To date, CG has incurred $4,400,000 in direct expenses including 76,220 direct labor hours. The project is running approximately 1 month behind schedule at this point. The CFO (David Oxner) has identified six options for recording revenue and profit in Appendix A. A summary of discussion with three separate auditors is provided in Appendix B.

Case requirements:

1. Group 1: Suppose your CFO proposes to adopt Option 1. How will this transaction be reported in your financial statements? What questions or issues would you like to have comfort on?
2. Group 2: Suppose your CFO proposes to adopt Option 5. How will this transaction be reported in your financial statements? What questions or issues would you like to have comfort on?
3. For both groups, please rate the three auditors on the scale below.

1	2	3	4	5	6	7	8	9	10	11
Very Poor Auditor				Average Auditor				Excellent Auditor		

Auditor 1   ______________

Auditor 2   ______________

Auditor 3   ______________

Case Appendix A

Six Revenue Recognition Options

1. Based on direct expenses:
   (4,400,000 / 53,000,000) × 1,600,000,000 =
   1. Revenue = $132,830,000
   2. Construction management fee margin = $ 2,768,000
2. Based on direct labor hours:
   (76,220 / 720,000) × 1,600,000,000 =
   1. Revenue = $169,377,780
   2. Construction management fee margin = $ 3,536,000
3. Based on total subcontractor costs incurred to date:
   (314,000,000 / 1,513,600,000) × 1,600,000,000 =
   1. Revenue = $331,923,890
   2. Construction management fee margin = $6,920,000
4. Based on total billings submitted to date:
   (338 / 1,600) × 1,600,000,000 =
   1. Revenue = $338,000,000
   2. Construction management fee margin = $7,055,752
5. Based on number of months of work completed:
   (9 / 36) × 1,600,000,000 =
   1. Revenue = $400,000,000
   2. Construction management fee margin = $8,320,000
6. Based on number of months work has been in progress:
   (10 / 36) × 1,600,000,000 =
   1. Revenue = $444,444,444
   2. Construction management fee margin = $9,280,000

Case Appendix B

Auditor 1

The issues in this case were discussed with Auditor 1. The response of
Auditor 1 was as follows:

> I was very comfortable with the existing revenue recognition pol-
> icy where percentage complete was based on total subcontractor

costs incurred to date (Option 3). However, circumstances have clearly changed with this new type of contract, and GAAP allows management to exercise judgment, so there is a range of possible outcomes that could work in this case. Option 1 is a conservative judgment, so I am willing to sign an unqualified opinion if this option is chosen. Option 5 is the maximum limit that could be recorded in this case with an unqualified opinion.

Auditor 2

The issues in this case were discussed with Auditor 2. The response of Auditor 2 was as follows:

> I was very comfortable with the existing revenue recognition policy where percentage complete was based on total subcontractor costs incurred to date (Option 3). However, circumstances have clearly changed with this new type of contract, so management can make a case for changing how the percentage complete will be determined for this new type of contract. The auditor has to determine the whether change results in better reporting (i.e., is preferable). This determination can be done at year-end after all the documentation required for the transaction is in place.
>
> A shift in how percentage completion is calculated for this type of contract should be disclosed in a note in the financial statements. This note could attract the attention of the Securities Commission staff. The Commission staff, in turn, may deem it to be an accounting policy change. If this happens, a major restatement of the financial statements may be triggered.
>
> Option 1 is a conservative judgment, so I am willing to sign an unqualified opinion if this option is chosen—though I want to reiterate that this could trigger an accounting change requirement from the Securities Commission staff (and possible restatement). The Commission staff will want the best estimate of revenue, but not necessarily a conservative estimate. There is a range of possible options, and Option 5 is the most aggressive option possible that could be recorded in this case with an unqualified opinion. Option 5 may, however, also trigger an accounting change requirement by the Securities Commission.

Auditor 3

The issues in this case were discussed with Auditor 3. The response of Auditor 3 was as follows:

I was very comfortable with the existing revenue recognition policy where percentage complete was based on total subcontractor costs incurred to date (Option 3). GAAP requires a company to make the most accurate estimate of revenue earned, and total subcontractor costs incurred to date is a good basis for estimating revenue earned. In my opinion, Option 3 is most consistent with the guidance in the GAAP, though a good case could be made for Option 5 (number of months of work completed) as well.

There are two risks inherent in this case:

1. A change in calculation of percentage complete could be construed to be an accounting policy change. This would trigger note disclosure and a need for restatement in order to present prior-year and current-year financial statements on a consistent basis.
2. The Securities Commission could disallow the options favored by management (Option 1 and Option 5) and insist on Option 3. This could open up a messy dispute with the Commission in which the company may not prevail.

Option 1 is a conservative judgment, so I am willing to sign an unqualified opinion if this option is chosen. My advice would be to frame the accounting policy choice in terms of Option 3 (total subcontractor costs incurred) but then make an allowance for measurement uncertainties related to estimating total costs incurred on the project that takes the reported number down to (or close to) Option 1. I would also recommend that management look at the financial statements of other companies in the industry and document these policies as further justification. I would be happy to assist in accessing policies of other companies in the industry.

Option 5 is also possible as a good option, though in this case a note disclosure will be required to justify a different treatment only for this new type of contract. Internally, documentation should be developed to justify the choice, and the company should have copies of what other companies do on file as well. I would be pleased to assist in accessing policies of other companies in the industry.

Key Points

1. Accounting numbers are unlikely to be truly neutral. The real issue becomes the degree to which the financial statements reflect the economic reality of the organization.
2. Information and disclosure within financial statements is becoming increasingly complex. This increased complexity is causing a breakdown in common knowledge and is making it easier for sophisticated investors to profit at the expense of less sophisticated investors. Expanded disclosure potentially hinders transparency in financial reporting.
3. A change is taking place in accounting standards from an accountability-oriented, historical cost perspective (conservative) to a future decision making–oriented, fair value perspective (increased subjectivity and uncertainty).
4. Managerial incentives can lead to the unintended consequence of earnings manipulation.
5. The auditor alone cannot safeguard the financial statements from all potential bias.
6. The financial statements are the responsibility of management, who makes all of the final decisions with regards to disclosure and presentation.
7. The auditor cannot push management to follow best practices but can only attempt to prevent management from falling below the base requirements.
8. Auditors deal with identified issues through different processes. The process utilized may dictate the amount of guidance provided to management.

Steps for the Board

1. What were the major issues that were discussed with the auditors? Were the issues settled appropriately?
   - Ask management whether external advice was required.
   - Discuss with both management and the audit committee whether an acceptable agreement was reached among the auditor, management, and the audit committee. To what degree was the audit committee involved in this process?
   - Arrange *in camera* meetings between the external auditor and board members without the presence of management to encourage candid dialogue.

2. Were there any significant changes in accounting policies in the current year?
   - Ask management for a list of both new accounting policies and changes to the existing policies.
   - Have management explain the reasons for the changes in accounting policies and the appropriateness of these policies. What was the effect of the change in policy on the financial statements of the company?
   - Consult the audit committee and the auditors, if the change is considered a significant financial issue, as to the preferable accounting policy for the circumstance and the appropriateness and aggressiveness of management's chosen policy.
   - Review the changes in accounting policy and current policies to determine whether the entity is conforming to industry standards and how aggressive the policies are overall and in isolation.

3. Are there areas where future-oriented, fair value accounting is utilized? Does management have access to high-quality information upon which to base its estimates?
   - Ask management to identify areas where fair value information is used within the financial statements.
   - Assess the appropriateness of the use of fair value information. Does it help inform the users about the economic situation of the entity?
   - Through discussion with management and the audit committee, gain an understanding of how the estimates of fair value are made. Assess the appropriateness of the estimation techniques utilized and evaluate your confidence level in these techniques.

4. What pressures do the organization's incentive plans place on managers to manipulate earnings?

   - Identify reported accounting figures that relate directly to financial targets used in managerial compensation. Scrutinize these figures with appropriate skepticism.
   - Discuss incentives in the organization that place pressure on managers to manipulate earnings without adequate mechanisms to control their behavior.

5. Does the firm meet industry standards for financial statement reporting and disclosure? Is the firm simply meeting the required standards or are their statements exemplary?

   - Ask the audit committee, external auditors, and management whether the company goes beyond simply meeting the requirements. Are they industry leaders in disclosure, accounting policies, and so on?

6. Does your auditor's approach to the resolution of accounting issues match with your company's and board's expectations and style?

   - Ask management and the auditor how they approach the resolution of accounting issues. Which process description do they align themselves with?
   - Assess management's ability to resolve accounting issues given the level of advice provided by the auditor. Is the auditor's guidance sufficient or overly aggressive given management's knowledge and attitude?

CHAPTER 2

Accounting as a Process by Which Financial Information Is Recorded

The recording function of accounting is a crucial part of the internal control system of an organization. Accounting tracks interactions among the organization and a variety of agents who provide goods and services to the organization. For example, the payroll system records contributions made by workers and processes their paychecks on a periodic basis. Likewise, the accounts payable system's function is to initiate transactions with suppliers (purchase requisitions) and then monitor supplier performance (including tracking, inspecting, and counting goods received from suppliers). The accounting system then processes supplier invoices and payments. The internal control function of accounting is indispensable to the proper functioning of an organization. An organization with poor internal control is vulnerable to theft or financial loss, both from insiders such as workers and outsiders such as customers and suppliers, and severe mismanagement of resources.

Most agents who interact with a company engage in short-term contracts and have personal knowledge about what contribution they provided, what their contractual entitlement is, and how well the internal control of the organization works. Workers and unions know a great deal about the actual work practices of an organization, its pay rates, the organization's ability to track number of hours worked, and compliance with overtime policies. Likewise, suppliers have a deep knowledge about how well the accounts payable system of the organization works. These agents do not have an interest in the quality of an organization's internal control system as long as they get paid on a timely basis. The agents do, however, have an interest in understanding a few key summary statistics about an organization. For example, net income informs all agents about the profitability of current arrangements. If net income is negative, this is a signal to all participants that current arrangements are unfeasible, and they should either exit the firm or expect to get less favorable terms in future contracts. A very high net income will tempt all agents to demand a larger fair share of the economic surplus generated. On the one hand, very high income will also attract the attention of politicians, unions, and various interest groups that could provide benefits. Examples are Boeing in United States, favored by the U.S. Department of Defense, and UBS AG in Switzerland, which continues to operate despite U.S. investigations into tax evasion. On the other hand, these parties could also do harm to the organization when they observe monopolies or organizations at the top end of their business cycles. Unwanted consequences of disclosure include the organization becoming a target for reduction in tax advantages or breaks for monopolists like Microsoft. All agents have an interest in understanding the liquidity of an organization. An organization that may go out of business can cause harm to all agents involved.

There is another class of agents who do not have direct personal knowledge of their entitlement to the organization. Shareholders and lenders often have a long-term commitment to the organization. For a business, the shareholders' entitlement is a combination of some tangible and intangible assets and liabilities. Accounting tries to create a representation of the shareholders' entitlement—that is, net income and shareholders' equity. To motivate managers to act in the shareholders' interest, managerial compensation contracts also give management a stake in the entitlement of the shareholders via profit sharing contracts. Unfortunately, these agents with long-term commitments to the organization have competing interests. Accounting standard setters thus have a difficult task of crafting "neutral" accounting standards.

Lenders provide capital to an organization but are then vulnerable to being defrauded by management's potential misuse of funds. Bankers thus prefer conservative accounting, which deliberately understates the true income of the organization. An understated, conservative income figure reduces what is available to other agents for their fair share of the economic income of the organization. Lower income reduces the amount of dividends that can be paid out to shareholders, the current tax payments to governments, and the union settlements to employees.

Some agents, like unions, may be able to partially overcome this bias by bargaining for benefits that are not reported or are poorly measured by accounting. The proliferation of defined-benefit pension plans, postretirement benefits, and stock options is motivated in part by the misreporting of these items in accounting, as they are often obscured in footnotes or absent from the financial statements. When changes are made to better report items such as pensions, stock options, and other postretirement benefits, we observe a significant reduction in the use of such items in compensation contracts. Bankers also have a keen interest in avoiding dilution of their claims. In addition to net income, bankers have an interest in ensuring that all liabilities of a firm are reported on the balance sheet. This demand makes it easier for a banker to protect her own interests by writing covenants based on Generally Accepted Accounting Principles (GAAP) numbers such as debt-equity ratios. The influence of bankers has created a conservatively biased historical cost accounting system, which lasted until the early 1970's. That system, as previously mentioned, is on its way out, as the interests of investors and management start to dominate the interests of bankers. The effect of fair value accounting will be discussed in more detail in chapter 6.

A Contract View of the Organization

It is useful to think of the various players both internal and external to the organization in relation to the contractual relationships and the reporting of the organization. Figure 2.1 provides a visual perspective of the interaction of these agents.

This diagram represents a view of the organization based on its contracting parties. It presents an overview of the organization for the board to obtain an understanding of the relationships between the organization and both its internal and external constituents. The arrows linking the various parties indicate that, under this contract view of the organization, each party contributes equally in a transaction. The diagram also provides a representation of the flow of information from the organization to these parties, which is hierarchical in nature. This hierarchy highlights

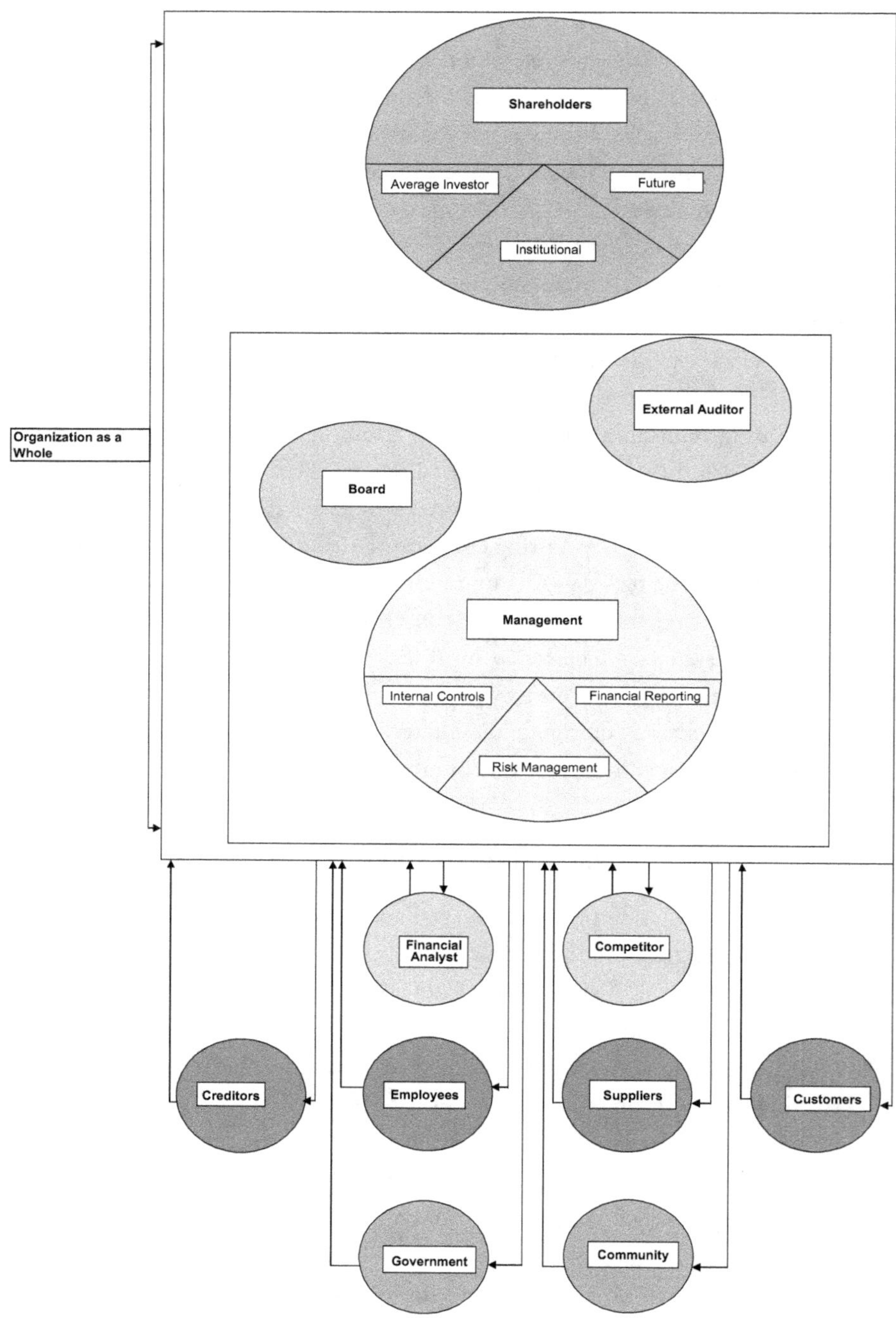

Figure 2.1. A contract view of the organization.

that parties have differing levels of access in the accounting information environment.

Of central importance to the organization and its financial reporting is management, which negotiates and renegotiates all contracts and is directly responsible for control over the information that is disclosed by the organization. Management establishes, implements, and operates the internal control, risk management, and financial reporting systems of the organization. These systems translate the actual state of the business of the organization into their respective accounting representations. The role of these systems is to gather information on the events that occur in the course of business between the various parties and to capture this information in a meaningful manner. It is then necessary for the systems to measure an event and possibly transform it into a form that can be used for reporting in the financial statements. The board should understand what is occurring in the business state in order to understand how this information is captured, measured, and transformed and how it is presented in the company's financial statements. The primary function of accounting is to create common knowledge between these agents.

The auditors and the shareholders are external to the organization, but the auditors have a direct link to management in sharing company information. Current and future shareholders rely on the board of directors and the auditors to obtain information about the status of the organization. The true picture of the organization is held by management alone, and the manner in which information gets presented to the other parties is primarily at the management's discretion.

In the lower portion of the diagram, we see the parties that are not part of the organization but that are linked to it through contracts. These parties have been presented in a hierarchical order based on their ability to access information on the organization. Competitors of the organization and financial analysts have been listed first in terms of this hierarchy. Due to their in-depth, expert knowledge of the organization and its industry, they are in the best position to both obtain and analyze the information that is disclosed and may have the clearest picture of the organization's actual business conditions. Next in the hierarchy are creditors, employees (union), suppliers, and customers. These parties may be in the best position to demand information from the organization because of their role in its operations and may also have firsthand knowledge of the business state of the organization.

At the bottom of the hierarchy are the government and the community. These parties have limited power to obtain information and insufficient incentives to process the given information. They are the most vulnerable to any selective and strategic disclosure practices by management. Although these parties may not have significant knowledge of the organization, this does not limit their ability to affect the operations of the organization negatively. For this reason, management may wish to build legitimacy in society through social responsibility disclosure, such as environmental reporting. In recent years, there has been an increase in the amount of disclosure in the annual report on companies' generous employment practices and their environmental activism.

Future contracting parties to the organization could be included in this last level of the hierarchy. Replacements may have to be found for the current contracting parties. These parties are future employees, future suppliers, and future creditors of the organization who currently do not have a direct link to the organization. The financial statements of the organization may be used to entice new parties to contract with the organization.

The Board's Role: Internal Controls

The quality of information transferred between parties to the organization is directly impacted by internal controls. The board, especially the audit committee, will have to understand and evaluate internal control over financial reporting. Financial reporting quality is the result of both internal control design and actual implementation. Controls are costly, can slow down interactions with customers, and can undermine employee morale. Therefore, control has to be used judiciously. Controls are often implemented by frontline personnel who may not understand the purpose of the controls and how to implement them properly. Management and the board will have to develop a policy on how many resources to devote to the design, training, and coaching of frontline employees about control.

Many organizations establish an internal audit department responsible for controls. One key decision about the internal audit department is the extent to which the internal auditors engage in preventive activities, such as design and coaching, as opposed to reactive activities, such as the detection of errors. The board will have to probe both the internal and external auditors to understand whether the right kind of control environment has been designed and whether the controls are being properly implemented.

Steering Your Board to the Forefront

One way to ascertain the orientation of the internal audit department is to ask whether the department participates in programs designed to enhance the organization's internal controls, such as control self-assessment (CSA). CSA is a program run by the Institute of Internal Auditors that seeks to promote good control by empowering frontline employees to understand control objectives. Under CSA, the internal auditors become coaches who help workers to design better control systems as opposed to being fraud or error detectors.

While it is in the best position to comment on the quality of internal controls and financial reporting, too frequently the external auditor is vague in reporting to the board on such issues. When the auditor is not forthcoming or precise regarding this evaluation, the board must probe the audit team. The highest level of precision when evaluating the quality of internal control and financial reporting would be obtained by applying a 100-point scale (or A–F scale). The external auditor has industry expertise and exposure to other clients within the industry and is the best positioned agent to determine these ratings. Unfortunately, external auditors are reluctant to provide quality ratings due to a litigious environment; at best, they provide a pass–fail rating. The board will need to further question the external auditor to obtain some sense of these ratings and determine whether the organization stands amongst others.

The board should also understand how the audit committee views the quality of internal control and the quality of the auditor. What attributes does the audit committee seek from the auditor?

In addition to reviewing the adequacy of internal controls, it is vital that the board try to get a sense of the prevailing attitude within the organization in regards to controls. It was stated previously that the actual controls are often implemented by frontline staff who have limited, if any, understanding of their purpose. The control culture within the organization is as important as the control procedures themselves. This message of proper controls must start at the board level so that all employees feel a sense that controls are important and understand why they are important or why they should care. If the employees sense that management is simply going through the motions with regards to control procedures, or that management is constantly finding loopholes in which to circumvent the rules, then they will follow suit and treat the controls as useless time wasters. The board must ensure that management is conforming to the controls that are placed on them and assess the attitude that management has toward the control system to foster a strong commitment to controls within the organization.

Overview of SOX 404 Certification

The Sarbanes-Oxley Act of 2002 (SOX) was passed in response to various accounting scandals. Of primary importance to this discussion is Section 404 of SOX. Section 404 requires that management and the external auditors report on the adequacy of the organization's internal control over financial reporting. This section has been highly controversial due to the cost of the requirements in terms of both effort and money. Both the external auditors and management are to perform a top-down risk assessment of the organization and focus their review of the controls to the high-risk segments of the organization.

From a board perspective, it is important for the board to review the internal control reports of both the external auditor and management. This review should include gaining an understanding of any control weaknesses identified and how management is addressing them. Is management's plan appropriate and adequate? It is also important for the board to understand the risk assessment procedure conducted by management and assess whether the risk assessments appear plausible. Essentially, management is identifying the areas for which the risk of misstatement or fraud is the highest. Management identifies accounts and processes for which this risk is highest in an attempt to focus its internal control review on these key areas and processes. To evaluate the plausibility of management's assessments, the board must utilize its knowledge and understanding of the organization to ensure that accounts and processes that are believed to have a high risk of misstatement and fraud are appropriately flagged by management. For instance, if the board is aware that one of the organization's key business processes is its sale of merchandise through subsidiaries, and it has identified this as an area for which management would have the ability to manipulate the financial position of the company, then it is important that management has also assessed this process as high risk. Any discrepancies between risk assessments performed by management, the auditor, and the board should be investigated and discussed.

Key Points

1. Management alone has the knowledge of the true picture of the organization's financial condition. Financial reporting involves a hierarchy with levels differing in terms of access to information.
2. The board must assess the risks faced by the organization and oversee the implementation and evaluation of effective controls to address these risks. SOX Section 404 includes measures to increase management's accountability with respect to internal controls.
3. The board needs to understand the quality of internal control and the quality of financial reporting of the organization. Ideally these quality ratings could be expressed on a 100-point scale. These ratings could be provided by the audit committee, the external auditor, or an independent contractor hired periodically to evaluate the quality of the internal controls.

Steps for the Board

1. How many resources have been devoted to internal control and audit? Is this the appropriate level?
   - Ask the external auditor whether controls and finance staff are adequate for the scope and complexity of the company's operations.

- Gain an understanding of management's risk assessment process. This can be done through discussion with the audit committee and management.

2. What is management's attitude toward internal controls? What is the board's attitude?

- Review the auditor's report on internal control deficiencies and any internal audit reports on the internal control process. Assess the appropriateness of management's actions and decisions. What is their prevailing attitude toward deficiencies and how does it reflect on their overall attitude toward controls?

- Have previous deficiencies been rectified by management? Are there deficiencies in internal controls that have been reported multiple times and that have not been addressed?

- As a board, discuss the level of internal controls that you feel are appropriate for the entity. Assess your own ability to set a high standard for internal controls at the board level.

3. What is the appropriate focus for the internal audit in regard to internal controls?

- Determine how much of the internal audit should be dedicated to the prevention as opposed to detection of errors.

- Does the organization participate in activities like CSA, where internal auditors act as coaches to help frontline personnel understand control objectives?

4. Was the right control environment designed for the organization?

- Question both the internal and external auditors on the adequacy of the internal controls.

- Ask the auditors and audit committee whether the controls are properly implemented.

- Obtain a rating of the quality of internal control (with the appropriate level of precision) from the internal auditor, external auditors, and management. Decide where the organization wishes to position itself in terms of adopting best practices.

CHAPTER 3

Accounting as a Process by Which Financial Information Is Classified

Accounting creates an elaborate system of classification. Account headings such as "sales/revenue," "gross margins," "research and development (R&D) expense" and "net income" have special significance to users of financial statements. Likewise, temporal classifications on the balance sheet between short term and long term are meant to convey different sets of meanings to readers of financial statements. Managers thus have incentives to manipulate the classification of items to achieve a favorable report of their activities. In some cases, a simple misclassification of current period expenditures from maintenance to R&D can be used to create a more favorable impression of the organization. In other cases, a multiperiod misclassification could be conducted to accelerate or delay the recognition of revenue in the current period's financial statements. On the surface, items such as cash or revenue appear to be simple enough. Most people are thus surprised to encounter a major fraud involving cash and accounts receivable or revenue recognition. In fact, these accounts can be extremely complex. How many times did Nortel have to restate its results before it figured out its revenue for the year 2001?[1] Also, Parmalat appeared to have loads of cash sitting in the bank over many years, until it was revealed that the balances of many subsidiaries (where discrepancies were easier to hide) had been forged.[2]

Let us look at the revenue for a food retailer like Safeway. This would seem to be a very simple business, yet Safeway has many possible sources of cash. For example, Safeway could generate a cash flow stream from the following activities:[3]

   a. Payments by retail customers when they buy groceries (about $44 billion in 2008).

   b. Promotional allowances provided by vendors to Safeway to promote their products ($1.95 billion in 2008). These can include promotions such as

      i. Temporary price reductions

      ii. Featured products in print advertisements

      iii. Featured products in the Safeway flyer

      iv. Placement of products in a preferred location in the store

   c. Slotting allowances provided by vendors to reimburse Safeway for cost of placing new products on the shelf ($130 million in 2008).

   d. Contract allowances where the vendor pays Safeway to keep a product on the shelf ($520 million in 2008).

   e. Vending machine sales

   f. Coupon redemption on behalf of suppliers

   g. Volume rebates from vendors

   h. The conduction of market research for vendors

   i. Point and loyalty programs

   j. Vendor exclusivity allowances

   k. Gift card sales

The variety of items used to generate cash flow raises a question about which of these items should be classified as revenue and which should be classified as reductions in the cost of goods purchased or as something else. These decisions have the potential to increase (or decrease) reported sales by several billion dollars per year. In the first instance, a company would have to identify the different streams of payments. Then an accounting policy would have to be adopted to distinguish items that are going to be classified as current period revenue (e.g., items a, f, h), deferred revenue (e.g., item k), reductions in cost of goods sold (e.g., items b, c, d, g, i, and j), or other (e.g., item e, as vending machine sales could be immaterial and classified as an "other" item). Classification will affect the revenue reported in the current period. Classification as deferred revenue will reduce revenue in the current reporting period but will increase revenue in a subsequent period. All increases in revenue will also increase the earnings for the period. Classification as a reduction in cost of goods sold will not affect the revenue figure but will increase the gross margin reported for the current year and increase the reported earnings. By classifying an item as "other," the item will not affect revenue but will increase reported earnings in the current period. Classification, therefore, has a significant effect on the line items reported on the financial statements and can also affect the income reported by the entity.

Since classification can affect the amount of revenue recognized in the current period, the cost of goods sold in the current period, as well as the amount of revenue recognized in future periods, it is important to understand which items of the financial statements are of significant importance to both the users of the financial statements and management. Benchmarking through the use of financial statement metrics will be discussed in chapter 5, but it is important at this point to understand how the use of accounting metrics can influence management's choice of classification. The key financial metric used to motivate management will affect their preference for the classification of an item. If, for example, management is evaluated based on the level of sales, or management believes that the stock price of the entity is contingent on the level of revenue, then management may have a bias toward accounting policies that maximize the classification of items as revenue. The board must be aware of these potential biases when evaluating the accounting policy and classification choices of management.

The Board's Role: Accounting Policy Formulation

The audit committee should be involved in the formulation of accounting policies. Once again, in this process, it should seek to understand industry conventions and best practices. The external auditor should assist in identifying the quality of the accounting policy proposed by management vis-à-vis best practices. The auditor could also help the organization disclose how different streams of cash flow are classified.

An organization can choose a policy to seek the most conservative reporting possible. For example, Microsoft has been accused of being too conservative by understating profits that might attract adverse political attention. An organization can also choose an aggressive policy or one falling between these two ends of the continuum. Once such a policy is adopted, it can continue to affect reported earnings over many years with no active decision making on the part of management or the audit committee on an ongoing basis. Since an accounting policy choice is a multi-period activity, reporting too much revenue in the current period means there will be less revenue to report in future periods. Likewise, reporting too little revenue now will lead to more revenue being reported in future periods. A conservative policy reports less revenue cumulatively over time. However, in any individual future reporting period, a conservative policy may cause reported revenue to be too high, too low, or about right in relation to the "true" revenue earned in that period. A director should understand the quality of an organization's accounting policies, since this is likely to be an enduring feature of the company. Directors should also be aware of politically charged accounting regulations, notably the expensing of stock option compensation and recognition of revenue, as these issues have received much public attention and regulatory scrutiny and may create a source of instability should the political agenda change.

Consider Nortel as an example for complex accounting policies. For a company like Nortel, it is unlikely that directors both on and off the audit committee can understand much of the detail of the accounting complexities the company faces. However, at a minimum, the directors should understand that the quality of internal control is inadequate for the size and complexity of the company; hence, they must make the constant restatements. The directors should also understand that Nortel's financial statements have always been very opaque and the quality of disclosure has been very poor. Even after all the scandals and the appointment of a new ethics officer, the quality of disclosure continues to be poor and Nortel's financial statements continue to be opaque. The Securities and Exchange Commission (SEC) enforcement action against senior managers of Nortel alleged that Nortel had a history of being too conservative in booking reserves.[4] Reserves were always booked on a worst-case basis to create a "cookie jar." Then reserves were released (i.e., cookies were consumed from the jar) as needed to meet earnings targets. The SEC contends that financial analysts and other users of Nortel's financial statements were aware of these reporting practices. Board members of Nortel ought to also have known that this excessive reserve-booking policy was a standard practice at Nortel and that the excessive conservatism could be seen as a pattern of manipulation rather than prudent reporting. The

SEC also alleged that Nortel used a "bill and hold" revenue recognition method (i.e., billing the customer for sales while goods were still on Nortel's premises) that was not in compliance with U.S. GAAP. The board should have at least been aware that the company used this method and that this was an aggressive revenue recognition method.

The Nortel example also highlights that regulators, especially the SEC, tend to primarily examine classification issues such as revenue recognition. Investigations of revenue recognition are a major source of accounting restatements. Regulators are also vigilant in conducting investigations of restatements and ensuring that they are substantiated by the need to correct errors or changes in accounting policies rather than to boost income and manage earnings.

Steering Your Board to the Forefront

The board can use analytical tools to assess the accuracy of its financial reports. Quality of income analysis, or earnings quality analysis, is based on the premise that high-quality earnings have a high correlation with cash flows. Furthermore, cash flows are more difficult to manipulate than income; hence, comparing cash flows with reported income should reveal aggressive or conservative use of accounting accruals. The ratio commonly used to measure earnings quality is,

Quality of Income = Operating Cash Flow ÷ Net Income

A ratio exceeding one normally indicates high-quality income, while a ratio less than one indicates problems with the quality of income. If the operating cash flow is negative and net income is positive, the ratio serves as a red flag, indicating poor earnings quality. Indeed, if the ratio shows problems with the quality of income, the next step is to conduct an in-depth cash flow analysis to determine how operating cash flows are generated. In the case of Sunbeam Corp., for example, the quality of income ratio fell from 1.61 in 1995 to –0.06 in 1996 (the year "Chainsaw" Al Dunlap was hired).

Key Points

1. The classification of items in the financial statements is one key area for potential manipulation that can cause great confusion for financial statement users. Classification involves the description of an amount, distinction between the short term and long term, and/or timing of recognizing an amount.

2. Excessive conservatism does not equate with prudent or neutral accounting.

3. Revenue recognition is the most common classification item targeted by regulators, notably the SEC, in enforcement actions.

Steps for the Board

1. Is the company a leader or a follower with regard to the quality of its accounting policies?
   - Question both management and the external auditors about the quality of the accounting policies of the firm as a whole.

2. How conservative or aggressive are the accounting policies of the organization (especially revenue recognition)?
   - Review the entity's major accounting policies. Determine whether they favor early recognition of revenue or deferral of expenses.
   - Review the policies to assess whether there is a trend or an overall bias.
   - Assess the quality of the organizations accounting policies and disclosure.
   - Obtain from the auditors and audit committee their assessment of the quality of the accounting policies and disclosure.

3. Are there any better accounting policies that the organization should be adopting?
   - Ask for a list of cash flows and their classifications (i.e., as revenue, deferrals, or those recorded elsewhere as a reduction of COGS or other).
   - Ask for a list of all off-balance-sheet debt and understand both the nature and dollar magnitude of the items involved.
   - Review the above listings for items that appear to be reported in a nonintuitive manner. For these items, question management, the audit committee, and/or the external auditor as to the appropriateness of the accounting treatment.

CHAPTER 4

Accounting as a Process by Which Financial Information Is Summarized

Accounting serves an aggregation function. The many millions of sales transactions at Safeway stores all over the United States and in various Canadian provinces are added together only on one dimension: the dollar amount. When Safeway reports a revenue number on its income statement (e.g., $44 billion in 2008), the company is providing a summary statistic that creates some useful and common knowledge among all users of Safeway's financial statements.[1] Note that this aggregation function helps users understand the magnitude of Safeway's revenue by suppressing a multitude of details about each sales transaction.

Reporting the sales number on the income statement is not sufficient to create transparency. To create transparency, Safeway will need to provide a very clear revenue recognition policy note disclosure (to indicate how items a through k in chapter 3 were classified) and several possible segment disclosures where sales may be broken down by geographical location (United States and Canada), type of cash flow (items a through k, discussed in chapter 3), department (bakery, pharmacy, meat), or some other dimension that management uses to make operating decisions.

Given advances in computer technology, it is possible to speculate that, in the future, Safeway and other companies could provide a database of all sales transactions and let the users create whatever data breakdowns interest them. Financial analysts would be the main constituency to benefit from such disclosure, other than competitors, and may be the only constituency that knows how to use and analyze the data provided in such databases. The detailed disclosure proposed here suggests that eXtensible Business Reporting Language[2] (XBRL) falls short of providing additional transparency, as it only serves a mechanical efficiency function that allows users to perform electronically the analyses that they would otherwise perform manually. The proposed move toward more detailed, computerized disclosure in the notes to the financial statements is hard to object to. A move toward providing databases of transactions can only be resisted if it provides too much information to competitors, who will probably be best positioned to understand the data disclosed, or to other agents who might use the information to attack the company, such as politicians or unions.

One source of financial reporting risk comes from companies increasingly striving to move an item off the financial statements such that no summary statistic is provided, causing the reader to be presented with a huge volume of note disclosure that provides very detailed descriptions of various features of a transaction. This is essentially the problem of "off-balance-sheet" debt. Many leases are now reported "off balance sheet" with no summary statistic in the financial statements. Should we worry about this accounting treatment, or is the transaction still transparent? For example, a lease can be structured as a capital lease, which is shown on the balance sheet, or as an operating lease, which is "off balance sheet" but disclosed in a note to the financial statements. For 2008, Safeway's disclosed Future Minimum Rental Payments for Leases were the following:[3]

Year	Capital Lease (On Balance Sheet)	Operating Lease (Off Balance Sheet)
2009	$94.3 million	$469.3 million
2010	86.9	438.4
2011	79.1	397.0
2012	74.8	365.6
2013	72.4	327.8
Thereafter	629.8	2,383.4
	1,037.3	4,381.5
Less: Interest	(480.1)	
Present value of minimum lease payments	557.2	
Less: Current obligation	(40.6)	
Long-term obligation	516.6	

How much lease-related debt does Safeway have? The board should at least be aware of the items that are off balance sheet and their dollar magnitude. Sophisticated users of financial statements (e.g., analysts, competitors) can construct their own models and read the note disclosures to create their own aggregate numbers. In addition to adjusting for off-balance-sheet debt, these users sort through the financial statements and remove some of the mechanical numbers created by accounting (e.g., depreciation) and adjust accounting numbers they think are not properly specified (e.g., pension liabilities). Academic research evidence suggests that even sophisticated analysts have a very limited understanding of accounting and probably cannot disentangle the aggregation function performed by management. If the note disclosures are very clear, these users can still only partly reproduce the aggregate numbers that would have or should have been produced by management. These users are thus disadvantaged even if the clarity of the notes is very good. As the clarity of the notes declines, the ability of these sophisticated users to understand the activity of the company will further decline.

Less sophisticated users of the financial statements are clearly worse off without the right balance of aggregation and disaggregation. These users lack the sophisticated models and ability to create an aggregation function and make adjustments to reported accounting numbers. They are faced with many pages of very detailed note disclosures that they don't know how to aggregate. They are drowned in incomprehensible details that they cannot process. In some cases, they also lack a summary statistic that is known to all users. Banks and other users are in a vulnerable position when an organization's financing is presented off balance sheet, as it enables organizations to relax the covenants attached to loan agreements and makes GAAP-based accounting numbers less useful as a means of constraining managerial behavior.

Aggregation Issues: Fair Value Versus Historical Cost

Accounting aggregation provides a useful summary statistic that, if skillfully decomposed and disclosed in the notes to the financial statements, creates good, transparent disclosure. The provision of a summary statistic also creates common knowledge across a range of agents and does not leave unsophisticated agents completely at the mercy of sophisticated agents. The aggregation thus helps create a more level playing field. Provision of the aggregate number should not, however, be used as an excuse not to provide good, clear note disclosure. Likewise, even the best note disclosure should not be seen as an adequate substitute for creating an aggregate number on the financial statements. Transparency requires both the aggregation on the financial statements and the decomposition in the note disclosure to both explain how the aggregation was done and partially undo the aggregation by providing various segment disclosures.

Aggregation can, however, also be problematic and meaningless. For example, let us look at the "Land" account on Safeway's balance sheet.[4] On December 31, 2008, Safeway had 1,739 retail stores, 382 fuel stations, 20 manufacturing and processing plants, and 17 distribution warehouses in the United States and western Canada.[5] Every year Safeway may buy land in some of the territories in which it operates. Under historical cost accounting, Safeway bought land for ($ in millions):

$996.2	prior to 2000
89.1	in 2000
132.0	in 2001
131.4	in 2002
36.9	in 2003
11.1	in 2004
17.9	in 2005
174.0	from 2006 to 2008
$1,588.6	2008 balance for land

Now, what does this $1,588.6 million amount on the balance sheet mean? Literally, it is just the net sum of all land purchase transactions over the life of the company. A dollar spent 20 years ago to buy land in Vancouver is treated the same as a dollar spent last year to buy land in Winnipeg. Certainly, this is not the value of the land owned by Safeway. The actual market value of the land could be many magnitudes higher. This is one of the limitations of historical cost accounting. While it is easy to audit this number, and hard for management to cheat, the number is also not meaningful to any reader of the financial statements. This is part of the reason for fair value accounting. Under fair value accounting, the company (i.e., management) would hire an appraiser. Suppose the appraiser said the market value of these properties is in the range from $19.5 billion to $22 billion. Reporting a number in this range would be far closer to the true value of the land (as compared to the historical cost of $1.6 billion); however, we have now opened up a discretionary judgment (estimate) of $2.5 billion that management can manipulate depending on their need for extra income in the current year. A potentially longer term risk is that once a company starts counting "unrealized" gains as income, governments might decide to start taxing the unrealized income—why wait for realization?

We could have the same problem on the income statement. After Safeway goes through a very detailed process of aggregating a variety of numbers to create an income statement (with a net income amount of $986.3 million in 2008),[6] the company decides that this net income amount is not meaningful. Safeway then disaggregates the net income number to create an EBITDA number (earnings before interest, taxes, depreciation and amortization). The idea is to show the earning power of the firm before debt charges and a variety of noncash expenses created by accounting (e.g., depreciation and amortization). If a large amount of financing is off balance sheet, then the cash flow available to service debt may be a useful summary statistic for lenders and other users of the financial statements. For fiscal 2008, Safeway's EBITDA numbers ($ in millions) are as follows:[7]

Net income	$965.3
LIFO expense	34.9
Interest expense	358.7
Depreciation	1,141.1
Stock options	62.3
Property impairment charges	40.3
Equity in unconsolidated subs	2.5
EBITDA	$3,144.5

The Board's Role: Select an Appropriate Level of Aggregation

The board should consider various levels of aggregation and examine the trade-off between measuring an item at historical cost as opposed to fair value. Historical cost accounting creates a meaningful income statement but treats the balance sheet as a residual of the income statement. This makes the balance sheet partly mechanical and sometimes distorted, like the "Land" account for Safeway. Fair value accounting reverses this process. Fair value makes some balance sheet accounts meaningful but distorts and introduces tremendous volatility in the income statement. If organizations have specialized assets or liabilities, it is possible that fair value will put some items on the balance sheet at market value (mark-to-market), some at cost, and some will be mark-to-model (e.g., stock option expense). This inconsistency introduces a whole series of distortions in the balance sheet. Furthermore, fair value aggregates persistent, realized cash flows with nonpersistent, unrealized gains or losses. Having a mix of realized and unrealized gains in the income statement gives management considerable room to distort the income statement. Fair value thus undermines the integrity of the income statement, neutralizes the external auditor as a control mechanism, and makes accounting vulnerable to massive fraud. There is no true representation of the financial condition of an organization. However, the organization can still strive toward providing meaningful financial reports. In chapter 6, we will consider some ways in which we might get both a meaningful income statement and a meaningful balance sheet.

Key Points

1. Accounting reports an aggregation of millions of transactions that can provide a meaningful summary statistic for analyzing an organization but that also can result in a significant loss of detail. Reporting a number on the financial statements helps create common knowledge but is not sufficient to create transparency. To create transparency, the company must also provide a detailed note disclosure.

2. Historical cost accounting creates an accounting number that is objective and difficult to manipulate. However, this accounting

number does not reflect the true economic value of the item. Fair value accounting helps report a more accurate estimate of the item's value but gives management an opportunity to more easily manage reported earnings for their own purposes.

Steps for the Board

1. What is the level of transparency of financial reporting in the organization?
   - Ask the auditor and the audit committee their perceptions of the transparency of the financial statements.
   - Review the financial statements to assess how much information is recorded within the financial statements and how much is disclosed in the notes to the financial statements.
   - By reading the financial statements, determine how understandable they are as a whole.
2. Where are historical cost and/or fair market value reporting creating distortions in the financial statements of the company?
   - Review the major assets and liabilities of the company. Determine whether they are recorded at cost or fair market value. Assess whether the given treatment is the most informative to financial statement users. Does it reflect the economic reality of the asset/liability?
3. To what degree does management provide aggregation versus rely on note disclosure to convey information?
   - Upon review of the financial statements, assess the board's ability to understand the information disclosed in the notes. Is the disclosure vague?
   - Compare the company's disclosure with its competitors' disclosures. Question management, the audit committee, and/or the auditors about differences within the industry.

CHAPTER 5

Accounting as a Process by Which Financial Information Is Interpreted

Accounting provides the principal input in the process of evaluating an organization's performance. Accounting information is used internally to make resource allocation decisions and externally to assess an organization's growth and prospects. In this chapter, we focus on how board members can use accounting information to identify the ways in which the company makes money. With an understanding of the key drivers of the business, the board can determine its accounting information needs and demand that management report on those measures that allow the board to benchmark the organization against itself and its competitors.

Nonfinancial Performance Measures

Nonfinancial performance measures can supplement accounting measures and further the board's ability to benchmark the organization. While most directors would agree nonfinancial performance measures are important for the board to examine, information provided to the board on these measures is often inadequate.[1] These metrics may be more effective than financial ones at zoning in on important intangibles for the organization, such as social responsibility, innovation, and reputation. Furthermore, they can be included in the evaluation of management for compensation purposes and may mitigate the implementation problem of accounting that leads to earnings manipulation. The use of nonfinancial performance measures, however, remains challenging for organizations due to a lack of benchmarking data from competitors, as the following example illustrates.

A Benchmarking Example

Let us continue with Safeway's 2008 annual report as an example to compare against two competitors, Costco and Loblaws (a Canadian grocery chain). Safeway experienced moderate growth in 2008, and management appears to have met its goals for the year. Looking through Safeway's annual report gives an indication of six areas that drive the business. Management has chosen to focus on high-quality meat and produce, proprietary brands, proprietary consumer data, supply chain efficiency, controlling labor costs, and social responsibility. Safeway has neither disclosed the specific metrics nor their targets and achievement of those targets. Instead, readers must go into the detail of the descriptive sections of the annual report to identify the achievements that management has reported on and assume that these are measured in some way within the business. It is evident that the gross profit margin is important to Safeway management, and the report emphasizes the company's capability to control costs because margins for groceries are so low. Thus, Safeway attempts to attain supply chain efficiency through shrink control and an optimal product mix. Safeway also must manage its labor contracts because 80% of its workforce is unionized and management must pay attention to collective bargaining agreements, disputes, and work stoppages. Effective cost control in these two areas appears to be the primary source of Safeway's success in 2008.

Safeway's competitor, Loblaws, faced a challenging year in 2008, as it attempted to recover from disappointing performance in previous years.[2] Loblaws's management has established a short list of key performance indicators with targets to evaluate its performance. Unlike Safeway, Loblaws has explicitly reported its key performance indicators in a separate section of the annual report, including both financial and nonfinancial measures. This disclosure makes it possible for Loblaws's competitors to benchmark performance against the company. Loblaws also differs from Safeway in that it not only distributes food but also offers general merchandise, a drugstore, and financial products. Financial measures that are important to Loblaws include sales growth, the debt-to-equity ratio, cash flow, and return on equity. The company reports non–Generally Accepted Accounting Principle (GAAP) amounts in evaluating performance on these measures (i.e., items are added to or excluded from GAAP net income). Areas of management focus involving nonfinancial measures include customers' perceptions of freshness, private label sales versus other brands, on-shelf availability, and employee satisfaction. An additional success factor for Loblaws is its management of real estate, as the company owns most of its properties.

Another competitor of Safeway is the mass-merchandiser Costco. The company experienced an outstanding year in 2008.[3] One of the principal ways in which Costco makes money is through membership fees, and thus renewal rates are a key indicator of its performance. In 2008, Costco achieved great success with a membership renewal rate of 87%, which the company has experienced for the past 3 years. Other important drivers for Costco are supplier partnerships and inventory turnover. Due to the rapid turnover of its inventory, Costco is able to obtain financing through its vendors. Essentially, customers pay for their purchases before the company pays its vendors. Costco also has a private label and has set growth targets for sales of this label.

By examining Safeway's disclosure of the key drivers of its business and comparing the company with its competitors, we see that the information reported by Safeway is less transparent than that of its competitors about the key metrics used by management to make decisions and measure its progress. While average shareholders will have difficulty in making these assessments, we hope that Safeway's board has knowledge of the key success metrics monitored by management and knows how well management is doing on those metrics. The board should also be aware that Safeway provides less transparency than it competitors and must understand (or at least ask the question) why this is (or is not) the best reporting stance for the company.

A Note on Transaction Structuring

Some degree of transaction structuring is inherent in business. Cash flows could be hedged to smooth out the underlying "real" cash flow of the company. This will also smooth out the accounting earnings of the company. The easiest way to manage both short- and long-term reported earnings is often to manage the underlying operations of the company. Short-term manipulation of earnings can be easily done by accelerating (or delaying) the start of an advertising campaign or a research and development (R&D) project. Such management actions would be completely opaque to outside users of the financial statements. They also will not attract the attention of the auditor and will probably never be discussed by the audit committee. Long-term manipulation of earnings will require more drastic operating activity, such as not engaging in a particular class of transactions because they make income volatile (e.g., some types of R&D projects) or conducting a transaction in a peculiar manner to achieve a particular accounting objective. While it is often popular to claim that operating decisions are not influenced by accounting considerations, there is considerable evidence that many transactions are indeed strongly influenced by accounting considerations. The board should thus have a sense of how accounting considerations influence operating decisions of management and how aggressive management is in taking advantage of the reporting flexibility provided by accounting. The same caution also applies to tax planning.

In the past, Wal-Mart has been very aggressive in trying to reduce the state income taxes it has to pay.[4] First, the company created a holding company in Delaware called WMR Inc. to hold its trademarks. Subsequently, all stores paid a royalty to WMR. This royalty payment generated an expense in states that have a state corporate income tax and income in a state (Delaware) that does not tax corporate income. When some state tax departments started challenging this holding company arrangement as a sham transaction, Wal-Mart dropped this practice but adopted a new and more aggressive strategy. The new strategy had been developed by Ernst & Young, which also happened to be Wal-Mart's external auditor. Wal-Mart created a real estate investment trust (REIT) in Delaware, and the REIT started charging all Wal-Mart stores "rent" for their premises. A REIT requires at least 100 shareholders, so 114 senior executives of Wal-Mart became shareholders of the REIT with 1% ownership and zero voting control. A Wal-Mart subsidiary incorporated in Delaware owned 99% of the shares and had 100% voting control. Wal-Mart then paid these executives an extra bonus for their participation in the REIT. The financial press estimates that that over a 4-year period, Wal-Mart saved $350 million in state taxes. More recently, Wal-Mart has been engulfed in negative publicity and dogged by state tax audits (and a lawsuit filed by the North Carolina Department of Revenue) alleging that the REIT structure is a sham designed only to reduce taxes. The board should understand how aggressive the organization is in tax structuring and assess how likely the company is to be involved in a scandal or mired in tax audits.[5]

The worst kind of earnings management is done by manipulating the real economic activity of the firm.[6] Failing to undertake a positive net present value (NPV) project or carrying out a positive NPV project in a convoluted and more costly fashion to attain a more favorable accounting treatment are harmful to shareholders. These manipulations are opaque to outsiders and destroy real economic value. Another dangerous earnings management tool is the choice of accounting policy, which is discussed at length in chapter 3. Since accounting policy choices tend to "lock in" a company for a considerable amount of time, such choices can have considerable impact on what is reported in the current and future periods. Initial adoption of an accounting policy is thus a significant activity. The clumsiest type of earnings management is done by manipulating discretionary accruals (e.g., bad debt allowances) on a period-by-period basis. Having a "cookie jar" and intervening every year to manipulate what goes in (and out) of the cookie jar is the most short-sighted and clearest form of manipulation. When a company starts doing short-term accrual manipulation, it may signal that the management is less competent and lacks foresight about future period cash flows (e.g., Nortel). It is ironic that a "cookie jar" strategy (see chapter 1 for a description) often starts out by being too conservative. In later periods the "cookies" are consumed. The conservative start disarms the external auditor and is often rationalized as being cautious and prudent. When a policy proposal is framed by management as being conservative, the board needs to make sure its not an excessive form of conservatism or conservatism that reverses very quickly (e.g., a very conservative bad debt allowance judgment that will reverse in the next year). Excessive conservatism, and especially easily reversible conservatism, has the potential to be an earnings-management game.

The presence of hedging and transaction structuring means that the board (or the audit committee) will really have to understand the business and perform a broader risk management function rather than a narrow accounting function. It is quite likely that earnings management will primarily be done through the operations of the business rather than through accounting. The recent options-backdating scandal (e.g., those involving Pixar Studios, Brocade, and Research in Motion) shows that it is often easiest to manipulate activity outside the accounting system.[7] This approach is troublesome, given that the board (and especially the audit committee) would be focused on the accounting system and might pay less attention to actual business activities. Rather than just having accounting experts on the audit committee, the board may be better served by having a more diverse skill set on the audit committee. This will prevent a narrow focus on accounting and reporting and help the audit committee to analyze the functioning of the organization itself and the business decisions that are being made by management.

Key Points

1. Accounting information is used to articulate how the company makes money and to benchmark the organization against itself and competitors.
2. Accounting considerations can influence operating decisions and transaction structuring.
3. Tax-planning decisions may attract the attention of tax auditors and the financial press.

Steps for the Board

1. Where does the company make money?
   - Gain a good understanding of the business by seeking assistance from management or from outside consultants.
   - Review the financial statements to determine whether they help investors understand how the company makes money.
   - Identify key metrics for which accounting information is required.
2. Accounting often misreports or fails to report significant assets and liabilities. Are adjustments required for distortions created by accounting?
   - Determine whether executive compensation metrics need to be adjusted for accounting distortions (e.g., expensing of R&D,

mechanical computation of noncash charges such as amortization). Often times non-GAAP metrics (like Economic Value Added [EVA]) are used due to distortions created by regular accounting (GAAP) numbers.

- Determine whether internally adjusted metrics should be reported in the financial statements or other company disclosures to better inform the users of the financial statements.

3. How do accounting considerations influence management's operating decisions? What are the key accounting numbers used by management to run the organization and measure performance?

- Ask management what they believe are the key accounting measures used to track performance. Based on the board's knowledge of the business, assess the appropriateness of these measures.

- Ask the auditors specifically about the overall aggressive/conservative nature of the accounting policies with regards to these specific measures.

- Review benchmarking information to understand who management considers to be main competitors and how the organization compares on these benchmarks vis-à-vis its competitors.

CHAPTER 6

Accounting as a Process by Which Financial Information Is Communicated

Accounting should function as a language of communication. Communication implies the sender has a message she wants to send, and there is a recipient of the message who can understand the message. Increasingly, accounting fails to carry out this communication. The sender constructs a convoluted message with some combination of historical cost (which measures some items well, some badly, some mechanically, and some not at all) and fair value accounting (some mark-to-market and some mark-to-model, some discounted and some not). The sender also omits information as she continues to leave many items off balance sheet. The most glaring omissions are research and development (R&D), debt structured in the form of leases and commitments, and environmental liabilities many years out in the future.

An example of accounting's failure to communicate value is R&D. A manager who makes the right investment decision will be penalized by accounting because all R&D expenditures are expensed immediately by accounting, and no corresponding asset is shown on the balance sheet. Another example of a shortcoming in communication is brand value. Companies like Coca-Cola have important brand assets that will not be shown on the balance sheet. Microsoft's human capital and The Body Shop's community reputation will likewise not be shown on the balance sheet. As a third example, a manager who makes the correct economic investment decisions may be forced by accounting to report the actions off balance sheet (e.g., for purchase commitments, some leases, and some special purpose entities).[1] A bank that creates a hedge to offset an existing exposure may find the asset figure reported at cost and the corresponding liability reported at market value.

Managerial opportunism then makes things worse by moving some (often quite substantial) debt off the balance sheet. This absence of information is then followed by many pages of commentary in the notes, some of which is boilerplate disclosure.

Finally, there are the users. Most users cannot understand the financial statements, so financial reporting loses its ability to create common knowledge among participants. This puts unsophisticated investors at a disadvantage vis-à-vis more sophisticated users of financial statements. Lack of common knowledge also makes markets more unstable and helps create irrationally optimistic expectations ("bubbles") in markets. Labor and supplier contract renegotiation can also become unstable in the absence of adequate common knowledge.

Communication is supposed to be a two-way process. Once an action is taken by management and disclosed, the markets can react. The reaction can come from labor unions, suppliers, financial analysts, the press, politicians, and traders in financial markets. These reactions can then feed back into both the operating and disclosure decisions of management. Since competitors are one of the agents monitoring public disclosure, management owes a duty to current shareholders not to be too transparent in their financial reporting. This lack of transparency is not a significant problem with respect to accounting because accounting numbers are highly aggregated. When we talk about transparency in accounting, we are talking about such a highly aggregated level that it may be difficult for a rival to understand much about the underlying "real" operating activity of the firm. The board should keep in mind that the people who understand the company's financial statements the best are usually its competitors. Keeping this in mind will crystallize the notion that there is a limit to transparency, and too much transparency may be bad for shareholders.[2]

How do we square the circle of providing an accurate income statement and balance sheet? The key objective is to help investors understand how well the organization is being run. One solution currently being considered by accounting standard setters is to break out all financial statements into operating and financing activities. This proposed practice creates a useful distinction, and we support adoption of this reform. One of the oldest tricks in the book is to take in capital and present it as operating revenue.[3]

In addition, our view of the solution is that we should return to a "core" financial statement, which is a historical cost type of accounting. This core statement (Layer 1) would use an accounting aggregation function to generate numbers for the core financial statements. The resulting statement would include the items that can be most reliably measured and would be audited. We can then add additional "layers" to the financial statements that provide additional information that undoes some of the damage done to the balance sheet by historical cost accounting. Following would be Layer 2, which comes with a review report rather than a full audit report—that is, a lower level of assurance. For example, a database showing all the parcels of land owned by a company like Safeway, together with the most recent appraiser's report (Layer 2), can help supply some of the information missing from the balance sheet. Finally, we add Layer 3, showing assets and liabilities that are currently ignored by accounting, which comes with no assurance report. For example, Layer 3 can disclose information about items that suffer from severe limitations in accounting measurement methodology (like R&D). Alternatively, the financial statements could be presented with Layer 1 coming first. The reader would then be shown very explicitly the items where Generally Accepted Accounting Principles (GAAP) do a good job of measuring some activity, followed by accounts where GAAP create some distortion, and finally followed with the financial statements of many items that are currently ignored by accounting because the accounting system does not know how to put a reliable number on such activity (e.g., R&D, future environmental liabilities). Our proposed financial statements leave it to the reader to determine the trade-off between the objectivity of numbers and having a complete picture of the organization's financial position.

Financial reporting at Wells Fargo (a U.S. bank operating primarily in California) provides an example of how savvy financial statement readers can use layers to parse out the true financial picture of a company. For Q2 2007, Wells Fargo reported a 9% increase in net income compared to the same period last quarter. Its net income is largely attributable to $1.21 billion of net gains on residential mortgage-servicing rights. While this gain is aggregated on the income statement, in its notes to the financial statements, Wells Fargo has applied a U.S. accounting pronouncement that establishes a hierarchy for fair value reporting with three levels based on the subjectivity of inputs for arriving at the values: level 1 from quoted prices in active markets; level 2 from observable inputs such as prices for actively traded, comparable assets and liabilities; and level 3 from unobservable inputs based on management's estimates. It is evident in the notes that this net gain is made up of a level 3 gain on the mortgage servicing rights used to offset significant level 1 and 2 losses on derivative items. Clearly, the basis of measurement for the loss on derivatives is more substantiated than the value reported for the gain. While accounting standard setters like to use politically appealing terms like "fair value accounting" and try to create the impression that these earnings are coming from marking-to-market, often the marking is done to model and sometimes the models and assumptions are based on a dubious and self-serving set of assumptions. Warren Buffett, who is a major shareholder of Wells Fargo, has described fair value accounting as "mark-to-myth" and cautioned investors not to trust any of these officially reported (and audited) numbers.[4] "Layered" reporting on the levels of subjectivity of inputs allows financial statement readers to identify the presence or absence of concrete value in an organization.

Accounting is sometimes compared to cartography. A map can be made at a high level of abstraction (e.g., of the world) or at finer levels of detail (e.g., of a country, a province, a city, or a neighborhood). Different levels of abstraction are useful for different purposes. Accounting tries to force all levels of abstraction into one general-purpose set of financial statements. The numbers on the financial statements can be thought of as being the highest level of abstraction (or aggregation, like a map of the world). The accounting policy notes and segment disclosures are like maps of a country or city showing more details about the numbers shown on the financial statements. A transaction database can be likened to a more detailed map of each neighborhood. We need to be careful, however, not to carry the map analogy too far. A mountain doesn't change when we create a map of it. An organization, however, is reflexive. Once accounting measures the managers' and shareholders' entitlement and discloses it, outside agents, as well as the managers, react to the information. The argument that "we make the right decision and accounting just reports it" is unlikely to be literally true. Management and the board need to be cognizant about how a wide array of agents will react to the accounting disclosures and how management will adjust its operating decisions based on the feedback received. No organization can ignore the reaction of its constituencies to the information it produces and disseminates.

The Board's Role:
Consider Receivers of Communication

The markets cannot react to actions that are not taken or not disclosed. The danger is that profitable projects are not undertaken because of accounting concerns or broader concerns about how various market agents will react to a particular action. No matter how efficient markets are, they cannot communicate and discipline the non-actions of management. The board should understand how accounting concerns influence what transactions are undertaken, why they are undertaken, and how transactions are structured because of accounting considerations.

Communication of Estimates and Judgments

At year-end, management makes a series of "estimates" including bad debt allowances, earnings on pension plan assets, impairment of goodwill, and possible liabilities many years in the future (e.g., oilsands plants will potentially incur cleanup costs 30 years from now—what should they record now?). Accounting provides an option to make conservative judgments based on past experience (e.g., allowance for doubtful accounts), to make judgments based on management's view of the future (e.g., fair value accounting), or to simply record these items mechanically (e.g., goodwill) or ignore them (e.g., future environmental liabilities of oilsands plants).

The Board's Role:
Benchmarking of Estimates and Transactions

The board should have an understanding of what estimates have been made in the completion of the financial statements. They should also track prior estimates compared to actual numbers in order to assess the estimation accuracy of the managers. For critical estimates, they should clarify the reasonableness of the estimate and the underlying assumptions used to formulate the estimate.

Additionally, observing the judgments and estimates that management makes and comparing them to industry practice and best practice can be very informative. When IBM got into trouble in the early 1980s, the first external sign of their difficulties was a change in the estimates of the useful lives of assets made by management to reduce the depreciation expense of the company. Likewise, a bank that makes very aggressive judgments of its loan-loss reserves is making its money in accounting, not in the underlying business. The board should understand the key accounting metrics involving judgment and estimation that management uses to run the business and measure its own performance. For these key metrics, the board should understand how conservative or aggressive the company's estimation approaches are and benchmark the company with its competitors and others in the industry.

Corporate Disclosure

An integral part of the process by which an organization communicates to stakeholders is through accounting disclosure. The previous chapters of this book have emphasized the importance and consequences of an organization's disclosure choices. The goal of this section is to summarize the ideas on disclosure that have been presented, as well as to introduce perspectives that directors should consider when evaluating disclosure.

Corporate disclosure includes both mandatory disclosure (e.g., financial statements, footnote disclosure, management's discussion and analysis) and voluntary disclosure (e.g., management forecasts, press releases, Web sites). Mandatory disclosure also involves a voluntary, or discretionary, element in that decisions can be made within GAAP and securities legislation. The ability of managers to make within-GAAP decisions leads to differences when comparing one organization's disclosure to another's. An example of within-GAAP differences is segment reporting (IFRS 8 "Operating Segments") under which an organization provides additional details on revenues by breaking them down into different sources. This disclosure rule involves a discretionary component where management decides which segments to use. Different presentations include geographic regions, product or service lines, or some combination of these categories. The organization is supposed to disclose segments that management would find useful for decision making under the assumption that the same breakdown would be the most useful of other financial statement users. However, management could withhold disclosing the level of detail and precise combination of segments, as well as sensitive information that is gathered and used within the organization. Detailed or sensitive information could include demographic data collected on customers that management uses to track sales, which would reveal its competitive advantages and might offend both customers and financial statement users. In addition, these disclosure decisions are driven by a cost-benefit evaluation of the factors discussed in the following sections.

Corporate disclosure is an extensively researched area in accounting. As discussed in previous chapters, particularly in the diagram of the contract view of the organization (see chapter 2), shareholders (current and prospective) are only one of multiple parties related to the corporation for whom disclosure matters. However, the majority of accounting studies focus on the effect of disclosure on capital market participants, such as stock traders and financial analysts. These studies have found a correlation between voluntary or enhanced disclosure and increased stock prices, as well as more precise pricing. This is only a small subset of the observations on disclosure. Researchers use various methods to measure the quality and amount of disclosure[5] and observe several indicators to detect the effect of disclosure (e.g., stock return, cost of capital, bid-ask spread, analyst following).

Findings suggest a benefit in the capital market arena for improved and increased disclosure. Yet why doesn't every CEO and organization strive to reach the highest level of disclosure possible? Increasing disclosure entails a number of costs. There is the direct cost of resources expended to provide additional disclosure. Secondly, there is the cost of increased disclosure arising from increased complexity. Recall that one function of accounting is to aggregate the details of operations and individual transactions into a summary statistic that can be utilized to form an overall picture of the economics of the organization and evaluate its performance. Once disclosure increases, it heightens the complexity for users attempting to discern the organization's key metrics. Lastly, the stock market and debt market participants are not the sole users of the financial statements of the organization. Other internal and external parties identified in the contract view of the organization are also part of the disclosure environment. Thus, it is important that disclosure be reviewed to ensure that proprietary information that could be used by competitors, employee unions, or the government against the organization is not disclosed without consideration of the potential costs. For example, a company might attract investors by disclosing some technological advancement, but such disclosure could give away its strategic position to competitors. In other examples, disclosures of very strong performance might prompt employees and governments to demand that the organization spread its wealth. The oilsands projects in Alberta, Canada, have trumpeted the success and wealth potential of these operations, drawing the attention of environmental lobbyists and politicians who have antagonized the projects.

We saw in the Safeway example that disclosure of this company's benchmark measures is less transparent than that of its competitors. Does the opaque disclosure reflect a decision to save the cost of providing additional details, or is the company unknowingly depriving itself of the benefit of increased disclosure? It is essential for Safeway's board not only to recognize its comparatively low level of disclosure but also to understand whether it is beneficial or detrimental to the organization. Users often look beyond the numbers to other dialogue, and the manner in which content is presented, to evaluate the company. Especially when a company is being compared to industry peers, corporate disclosure is a mechanism of branding or marketing the organization.

Financial statement users must recognize an inherent limitation of disclosure: Even under the highest level of disclosure discussed in both accounting research and throughout this book, there is no mechanism for financial statement users to observe incidences where management has failed to take an action that would have benefited the organization (i.e., non-actions). This is a limitation of disclosure that can not be fixed by increasing the amount or the quality of information. Users can best navigate around this limitation by benchmarking an organization against its industry peers and leveraging the knowledge of board members to identify the organization's prospects. The board should recognize that information must be obtained in addition to accounting disclosure to ensure that management is not passing on projects that could benefit the company and its shareholders.

The Board's Role:
Assessing the Level of Corporate Disclosure

The board needs to have an understanding of the level of its organization's disclosure and develop a notion of quality. This assessment can be obtained through discussions with the audit committee, management, and the external auditor. Is your corporation a thought leader in disclosure practices? The organization might view disclosure as a strategic opportunity likened to any marketing communication. One on hand, perhaps your organization will choose to position itself as a thought leader in disclosure practices. On the other hand, when faced with enhanced disclosure decisions by management, the board must determine the cost of disclosure. The information might be of a sensitive nature—does it reveal information to competitors or employees that they might use to gain an advantage over the organization? The board should assess whether the risk and cost are worthwhile in relation to the benefits of enhanced disclosure.

Key Points

1. The objective of financial statements as a communication tool is to provide a clear picture of the organization's financial condition.

2. Disclosure comes at a cost, both in the direct cost of producing additional information and in the loss of proprietary information. On one hand, too much disclosure can be harmful to the organization. Care should be taken to ensure the increased disclosure benefits outweigh any potential costs due to the provision of additional information to competitors, regulators, unions, and others. On the other hand, accounting produces very highly aggregated numbers. Slogans of truth and transparency are not literally true in accounting. Accounting provides a very coarse representation of the economic state of a firm. For example, non-actions taken by management cannot be communicated through accounting reports.

3. It is not the interest of only the current shareholders that must be considered when analyzing the financial statements. All the agents that interact with the company have an interest in the profitability and liquidity of the organization.
4. The level of estimation that management has applied to an accounting figure is not clearly communicated in accounting reports.
5. By enhancing corporate disclosure, firms may be able to reduce their cost of capital by reducing the information asymmetry in the marketplace.

Steps for the Board

1. Is accounting a two-way process of communication?
   - Understand that accounting only provides a highly aggregated picture of the organization.
   - Review the disclosure of the entity and determine whether the key decisions of management are hidden from the markets due to this aggregation.
2. How aggressive is management in taking advantage of the reporting flexibility provided by accounting?
   - Ask both the auditors and management for a list of accounts for which significant estimates were made in the current year.
   - Compare the historical estimates and query both management and the auditors as to the degree of conservatism used in providing the estimates.
   - Ask both management and the external auditor about management's philosophy (and aggressiveness) about tax planning and taking accounting considerations into account when undertaking and structuring transactions.
3. Accounting figures range from those that have verifiable historical bases to those that are purely estimates. How concrete in nature are the financial statement numbers?
   - Ask management that financial statements be reported in order of "hardness" of the numbers.

4. Does the firm follow an optimal disclosure strategy? Does the cost of additional disclosure outweigh the benefits and is disclosure of sufficient quality?

   • Ask the audit committee, external auditors and management how the disclosure of the company compares to the industry leaders in terms of quantity and quality.

   • Is the information disclosed in an understandable format? Can the board members themselves understand the nature of the business and its transactions through review of the disclosure?

   • Ask the audit committee, external auditors, and management to specify the cost of additional disclosure quality and quantity to make the company a leader in their disclosure strategy. Does this cost outweigh the benefits?

CHAPTER 7

Current Issues in Financial Reporting

International Financial Reporting Standards (IFRS) and Transition for U.S. and Canadian Companies

The migration of accounting from a cost basis to a fair market value basis has been presented in previous chapters. In addition to this general shift in accounting standards, there is a harmonization of international accounting standards underway for U.S. and Canadian companies. The United States and Canada are moving to the adoption of IFRS for publicly listed organizations. This segment provides an overview of IFRS, the timeline for the adoption of IFRS, an overview of the conversion process, and the board's role in the conversion to IFRS.

IFRS Overview

IFRS are set by the International Accounting Standards Board (IASB), an independent, international body dedicated exclusively to the development of international standards in accounting and financial reporting. The IASB comprises 14 members, appointed and overseen by the International Accounting Standards Committee Foundation (IASCF). Individual members are selected for their expertise in standard setting, with the board as a whole representing global diversity and multiple perspectives.

IFRS are essentially a global set of accounting standards. IFRS are currently used in more than 100 countries and regions, including the United Kingdom, the European Union, Hong Kong, and Australia, and is accepted as a standard of reporting by the United States Securities and Exchange Commission (SEC) for foreign filers without reconciliation. It is seen as a high-quality set of standards. The benefits of the adoption of a unified set of standards from a global perspective are a reduction in the reporting costs of multinationals, the provision of increased comparability, and the improvement of capital allocation by investors.

Timeline for Convergence

Countries with significant capital markets around the world are continuing to publish their proposed roadmaps for adoption of IFRS. These roadmaps apply to publicly held enterprises (recall that accounting for private entities was discussed earlier in this book). Canadian Generally Accepted Accounting Standards (GAAP) require that all for-profit Canadian entities file their financial statements in conformance with IFRS by 2011. The United States is working toward convergence in 2014. Japan and Korea's adoption is proposed for 2011. Taking these dates as the deadlines for the company conversion, entities in these countries should be implementing, or at least developing, a conversion plan at present. This conversion plan should include the timeline and budget for conversion as well as a list of significant conversion issues. As a board, it is important to identify the stage of conversion to which the organization has progressed.

American entities filing on the U.S. stock exchanges currently do not have a deadline for total conversion to IFRS. For U.S. entities, the Financial Accounting Standards Board (FASB) is in the process of converging U.S. GAAP with IFRS through short-term projects dealing with specific GAAP topics. Foreign entities filing on these stock exchanges are allowed to file their statements in conformance with IFRS, but U.S. entities are currently required to file under U.S. GAAP. There is speculation that U.S. entities will be permitted to adopt IFRS prior to a set deadline. Early adoption may allow for a company to gain a competitive head start. With the downturn of the economy beginning in 2008 and the increased competition for capital, a competitive advantage may be valuable vis-à-vis the costs of conversion. Adoption of IFRS might also allow for more streamlined reporting for entities with significant foreign reporting requirements. The boards of companies in the United States and other conversion countries should keep a close eye on the regulatory developments to determine when early adoption becomes available. The board should also require management to investigate the advantages of early adoption for their entity in order to develop a preplan for conversion. U.S. American Institute of Certified Public Accountants (AICPA) members polled indicated that it would take 3 to 5 years to prepare for IFRS conversion. Given this timeline, the board needs to address the issues of conversion earlier rather than later.

Implementing the Conversion

The Canadian Institute of Chartered Accountants (CICA) has provided Canadian companies with a detailed plan for the adoption of IFRS.[1] The steps for the CICA plan are beneficial regardless of your jurisdiction and are briefly detailed as follows:

1. Appoint a project team.
2. Learn about IFRS.
3. Assess the impact of IFRS on your specific situation.
4. Assess your options under IFRS 1 "First-time Adoption of International Financial Reporting Standards" (there are some allowable options for first-time filers).
5. Begin to draft your plan.
6. Communicate with your board, your auditors, your investors, your lenders, your employees, and other stakeholders.

The detailed steps for conversion will be carried out by management, but it is important for the board to understand this process and monitor management's progress.

The Board's Role: Review of Conversion to IFRS

As articulated in chapter 3 and throughout the remainder of the book, it is important for the board to understand the accounting policy choices of management. The conversion to IFRS brings about a large number of policy choices for management. It is imperative that the board review these choices of management in the same critical manner that they would all other accounting policy changes. When a large scale conversion occurs such as that required by Sarbanes-Oxley (SOX), and now by IFRS adoption, it is critical for the board to keep a watchful eye on the choices made by management.

The board must also attempt to ensure that the conversion to IFRS goes as smoothly as possible. This entails ensuring that management has an adequate plan for conversion. Based on the CICA steps for IFRS conversion planning presented above, the board should review the plan to ensure that the project team is properly educated in IFRS and has sufficient knowledge of the entity to plan and execute the conversion. The board should review the team's assessment of the impact of IFRS on the entity and question the audit committee on any significant and unresolved items. IFRS conversion may affect the reported earnings of the entity and the board needs to be aware of the impact on financial reporting.[2] Contractual agreements may need to be modified as a result of these changes. Debt covenants, lending agreements, and bonus-based remuneration plans are just a sample of the agreements that may be impacted by the conversion to IFRS. The board should also review the overall conversion plan to ensure that there are sufficient resources available to meet the conversion deadline. Although no one expects the board to be experts in IFRS, it is imperative that directors understand what the company is doing to convert to IFRS and seek external advice should complex IFRS issues arise.

From the Stock Exchange to the Local Boardroom: Private Companies and Small Businesses

One of the prevailing ideas in accounting is the desirability of having one common set of accounting standards for all organizations. For publicly traded companies, there are large differences in the underlying nature of economic activity across industries and even within an industry. Thus one source of debate in the accounting literature is about the wisdom of requiring all publicly traded companies to follow the same set of accounting standards. More likely, however, is the potential for distortion to arise from forcing private companies, not-for-profit entities, and government organizations to follow the same standards as those developed for publicly traded organizations. This segment focuses on accounting for small business enterprises.

Small Business Enterprises Are Different

There is currently a movement within the small business community to push standard setters away from a one-size-fits-all approach to accounting regulations. This would allow differential reporting requirements for entities that meet specified criteria. The move to fair value reporting is putting unrealistic and unnecessary reporting requirements on companies where all investors are well informed of the operations and successes of the organization. These enterprises, often referred to as small business enterprises (SBEs), are characterized as having financial statement users that are few in number and are more concerned with stewardship (accountability). They do not include publicly listed enterprises, cooperative organizations, pension plans, or financial institutions.

An Illustrative Case

The new reporting requirements have become increasingly complex and require a substantial investment by the organization in order to be implemented. Due to the stewardship focus of the users of SBE financial statements, there is little benefit derived from this increased complexity and expenditure of resources.

For example, let us look at the case of an organization that runs 40 pizza outlets in mall locations throughout the province/state. The organization is owned solely by one family with no outside ownership. The organization's only outside user of its financial statements is the bank that holds its debt. Since the organization operates in 40 locations, it holds leases with various strip malls throughout the province/state. These leases of premises are long term in nature, extending anywhere from 1 to 30 years depending on the location.

The financial instruments section of GAAP requires a company to recognize any asset or liability that is contained within any of their lease contracts. These are referred to as embedded derivatives. Basically, an embedded derivative within a contract is an asset or liability that is caused by a benefit or loss that is expected in the future due to the terms of the contract. Although this rule sounds quite involved and some what obscure, if we go back to our pizza restaurateur, we can easily see how it may pose a problem. The 40 leases that this organization has entered into may result in some future economic benefit or cost to the organization. If the market rent for the mall has increased in relation to the lease rent, then the organization is holding a future (economic) gain resulting from the difference between the market rent and their actual lease rent. On the other hand, if the market rent for the mall has decreased in relation to the lease rent, then the organization is holding a future liability within this lease caused by the difference between the market rent and the lease rent.

The question for this nonpublic organization that is closely held is whether the disclosure of this potential liability or asset be beneficial to the users of the statement? The cost of producing this disclosure in the financial statements could be significant in that the organization and the auditors would have to examine each of the lease arrangements and obtain estimates of potential hypothetical market rents and an estimate of expected future market rents for each of the locations to assess whether an asset or liability exists. Now imagine the work required if they held 900 leases for premises and equipment. The bank and the owners themselves are likely more concerned with the future actual cash requirements caused by these leases than they are about the differences between the hypothetical market rents in the future and current lease rents.

Differential Reporting

Regardless of whether a country has adopted IFRS, national regulators (rather than the IASB) govern whether organizations that qualify as SBEs may follow differential reporting requirements. Some jurisdictions allow SBEs to elect to follow differential reporting standards within GAAP, while others require one set of GAAP for all organizations. The use of differential reporting basically allows these organizations to avoid some of the more complex accounting rules, specifically in areas where rules are not seen to add a substantial benefit in disclosure for the organization versus the cost of compliance. In the United States, the United Kingdom, Canada, and Australia, the scope of differential reporting may even apply to nonpublicly listed entities that are quite large. It is important to note that, for organizations that adopt differential reporting, the principles of GAAP continue to apply.

The use of differential reporting is meant to provide meaningful reporting without the cost of unnecessary complexities in areas where very detailed rules do not add usefulness to financial statement readers. For example, Canadian GAAP allows for the organization to elect differential rules in five specific areas. The organization can, thus, choose to follow differential reporting for all or any combination of these areas. This results in the potential for a different combination of standards for each organization. In order to utilize differential reporting, the organization needs unanimous consent from all owners of the organization, both voting and nonvoting. The areas of differential standards in Canada are as follows:

- The treatment of long-term investments (subsidiaries, joint ventures/cotenancies)
- Income taxes
- Share capital
- Fair value of financial instruments
- Goodwill impairment testing

This list is not static. Committees in each nation review GAAP to determine whether new requirements should be included in the differential reporting list. These committees are charged with weighing the cost of the new requirement with the benefits to the SBE users of the increased disclosure.

Accounting Restatements

In a restatement, the organization performs a retrospective correction of the recognition, measurement, or disclosure of an item reported in the financial statements. Restatements are *not* warranted by GAAP when new information has been acquired to result in a change in estimates, such as a change in the fair value of an asset. In this case, a revision in the current period and going forward is the appropriate accounting treatment. A restatement can be initiated by management, the auditor, or a change in accounting standards. It is thus important for the board to understand who is initiating the restatement.

A restatement usually triggers negative press coverage and regulatory scrutiny. For example, the financial press coverage of the Canadian company Nortel may make the public wonder how many times the company will restate its accounting figures from 2000 onward. Nortel has explained that the restatements have primarily involved timing errors on the recognition of revenue, though it is not clear why Nortel has so much trouble determining its revenue for past periods. Boards should understand the conditions that necessitate restatement and implications of restating prior period figures, as well as the disclosures involved when an organization issues restated financial statements.

Restatements are a red flag to regulators who may view them as evidence of poor financial reporting practices and weak internal controls. Restatements may also be an earnings-management scheme used by managers to improve earnings. For example, management may be overly conservative in its selection of an accounting policy and later demonstrate that a less conservative policy is more appropriate, leading to increased income in a future period when the less conservative policy is adopted.

When restatements occur, financial statement users may suspect that management had information about the appropriate accounting policy in the period being restated and deliberately made an inappropriate choice. However, it is important to remember that restatements may be necessary for good financial reporting in the circumstances where an error was discovered or a different accounting policy provides the best accounting information. The organization must, therefore, provide adequate disclosure in the notes to the financial statements for users to understand whether the restatement is good or bad and to track management's true financial performance. In the case of Nortel, even a very careful reading of note disclosure makes it almost impossible for a reader to understand why the multiple restatements are taking place. This is a sign of poor-quality reporting that should raise concerns not only for regulators but also for shareholders, lenders, and, certainly, the board.

Key Points

1. Significant country markets report under IFRS while others have established roadmaps for convergence, some as soon as 2011. Due to the time and effort required, entities should already have a plan for conversion.

2. The conversion to IFRS by entities may result in changes to the earnings of the organization. These changes in earnings and in classification of some items may necessitate modifications to contractual obligations.

3. With GAAP moving toward a more fair value representation of the organization, the standards are becoming increasingly complex, particularly for smaller, privately held organizations.

4. SBEs with few financial statement users may be at a disadvantage due to complex regulations because of their focus on stewardship rather than future value and costs of implementing such accounting policies.

5. SBEs currently have the ability to use differential reporting to eliminate a small set of onerous GAAP requirements.

6. Accounting restatements draw the attention of financial statement users, particular regulators and the financial press. Since restatements might be necessary for proper accounting, adequate disclosure that describes why a restatement was issued conveys the organization's commitment to good financial reporting.

Steps for the Board

1. Does the entity have a detailed plan for IFRS conversion?
   - Review the plan by management for conversion to IFRS and determine whether it contains the elements suggested by the CICA guide.
   - Question the audit committee as to the sufficiency and feasibility of management's conversion plans.
   - Ensure that adequate resources have been committed to the conversion to IFRS.

2. Does the conversion to IFRS cause significant changes in the accounting policies of the entity?
   - Review the accounting policy changes caused by IFRS.
   - Determine whether management has chosen an aggressive or conservative position with regards to the changes in policy.

- Question the audit committee and the auditors about the appropriateness of management's choices on IFRS policies. Are they comparable with prior policies? Are they comparable with industry policies?
- Assess the impact of the changes in policy on contractual agreements. Discuss with management the need to renegotiate any contracts significantly affected by IFRS.

3. Is differential reporting being used within your organization?
   - Ask for a detailed list of all differential reporting standards being applied.
   - Confirm that the differential reporting standards utilized have been approved by all shareholders.

4. Where are differential reporting opportunities present and absent?
   - Ask whether the organization is expending a large number of resources to comply with any accounting standards that could be avoided through the use of differential reporting.
   - Ask management for an explanation of what the benefits of this disclosure are to the users of the financial statements that justify the decision not to use differential reporting.

5. Has the organization made restatements in past or present periods? Is it at risk for making restatements?
   - Ask management whether accounting policies have changed or whether new information has revealed accounting errors in past periods.
   - Ask about restatements, if any. Are the conditions for restatement met?
   - Assess what the cause of the restatement is and determine whether it is appropriate to take any corrective action with regards to the restatement.
   - Track the history of restatements by management to determine whether a pattern may indicate a potential problem, such as a problem with management integrity or a serious internal control weakness.
   - Question the auditor with regards to the potential cause of the restatement. Discuss with the auditor and/or audit committee whether they perceive the risk of misstatement to be indicative of a larger issue with management.

CHAPTER 8

Accounting for a Not-for-Profit Organization

A large portion of economic activity occurs outside of publicly traded corporations. It is thus likely that directors of public companies may also serve on boards of a host of nonprofit entities. In essence, a not-for-profit organization (NFPO) has no direct owners, provides no financial return to contributors, and the activities and objectives of the organization center primarily on the public good. The not-for-profit sector of the economy is significant and includes quasi-governmental organizations. Budgets in the not-for-profit sector can be significant, as is the case with the Edmonton Community Foundation in Canada, which had a total of approximately $223 million in assets in 2008 and cash expenditures of approximately $7 million for that same year. What this means for directors is that NFPOs can be diverse, complex organizations with substantial economic activity and important reporting responsibilities.

Differences Between For-Profit and Not-for-Profit Organizations

The primary difference between the NFPO and the for-profit organization (FPO) is its purpose or objective. For the FPO, its simplified purpose is to maximize the return to the shareholders. This goal encompasses maximization of profit and maximization of share price. In an FPO, there is a direct connection between revenues earned and cost of goods and services incurred. Net income has an economic meaning in this setting. In addition, a key source of discipline and feedback comes from the product market. If the goods (or services) provided by a company are not desired by market participants at current prices, the company will suffer a loss or a low profit. Likewise, pricing power and profitability are signals about the ability of the company to satisfy its customers within existing cost structures and return a profit to shareholders.

The NFPO's goals, sources of discipline, and feedback signals are quite different. There is no direct connection between the revenue earned and the cost or quality of the goods and services provided to clients (i.e., those who benefit from the NFPO's cause). Since the organization does not operate to earn money by charging clients who receive services, there is less market discipline or feedback about performance. Each organization will have its own purpose and its own goals relating to this purpose, but essentially it aims to provide the maximum services or benefits to its cause or clients with the maximum amount of resources they are able to obtain. If we take a hospital as an example, its goal is to service and aid as many patients as possible with the amount of funding that it has available. This will include maximizing the amount of funding it can obtain and perhaps maximizing the number of patients it serves. There are few, if any, signals about the optimal size or quality of a hospital (or a food bank—is it a success if more people use a food bank?). Decisions about capacity, funding, and service provision are more likely to be driven by political and nonfinancial performance metrics. The management and board of a hospital have to define what it means for the hospital to be successful. It is unlikely that a summary statistic created by accounting (e.g., net income) will be an adequate performance metric for a hospital. Lack of availability of such commonly accepted performance metrics makes governance of a hospital a much more difficult and complex process.

Differences Between Not-for-Profit and For-Profit Accounting

Generally Accepted Accounting Principles (GAAP) continue to apply to NFPOs. International Financial Reporting Standards (IFRS) were not designed to apply to NFPOs, so individual nations that have adopted or are converging with IFRS govern the standards that NFPOs are to follow. The first difference is in internal control. In an FPO, there is a correspondence between the provision of goods (or services) and receipt of cash. Improvements in internal control in regard to both efficiency and effectiveness of asset use translate directly into higher net income. This link is weaker or nonexistent in a NFPO. An NFPO must be concerned with efficiency and effectiveness of its control processes even though it does not have the ability to get clear feedback from a summary statistic like net income. Many large charitable organizations (and especially government organizations) carry out extensive "value for money" audits to assess and improve their internal control processes.

Recording and reporting in an NFPO context is potentially more complex than in an FPO context. If revenues are obtained from recurring and well-known sources of funds (e.g., a government grant), then revenues are relatively easy to recognize. If a fundraising campaign is organized, then controls will have to be placed over the recruiting, fundraising procedures, and receipt issuance processes to ensure that all donations made are properly solicited, received, and receipted by the organization. Since there is no direct link between receipt of funds and provision of services, it is much easier for a fundraiser to steal revenues in a NFPO. Unrecorded (or underrecorded) revenues are a major risk in NFPOs.

A second complicating reporting factor for NFPOs is that since revenues come from donors who care about the mission of the organization, cash received is likely to come with restrictions on their use. The organization cannot simply pool its resources and spend them as they see fit. Generally, donors will attach conditions to how their money can be used. For example, if a family gives money to a university and specifies that the funds should be used to provide a scholarship to a student studying law, then the funds must be used for that purpose and cannot be used to pay the operating expenses of the university. A university is thus likely to have tens of thousands of different "funds" that track the use of resources based on the purpose for which the money was given. This will make the internal accounting system of an NFPO (or government agency) much more complicated than that of an FPO. The financial statements of a university (or government) will be very voluminous, will lack a summary statistic (like net income), and will be very hard to understand in aggregate. It is quite common for large charitable organizations (and governments) to issue financial statements that are fragmented and several hundred pages long.

All the dollars that come into an NFPO (e.g., a university) for a given year can be aggregated and reported as revenue for the year. However, this number is unlikely to be meaningful to most readers of the financial statements, especially since use of these funds is legally restricted. Due to the difference in goals (and legal restrictions on assets) between NFPOs and FPOs, the readers of the financial statements will use them differently. While the FPO users will focus on a few summary statistics, such as net income and the liquidity of the organization, the NFPO users do not have such measures available. Instead, users will be concerned with how much funding was collected for each purpose, the source of funds, the cost of raising the funds (overhead), how the funds were actually distributed to each objective, and what measures indicate successful accomplishment of diverse objectives. Again, these success measures are likely to be nonfinancial in nature.

An appreciation of the differences in the use of the financial statement of NFPOs versus FPOs has led to the need for a different set of standards for NFPO.[1] Under IFRS, there is no separate set of GAAP for NFPOs. Thus, NFPO's have to follow the underlying principles that apply to FPOs. In countries such as Canada and the United States that have a supplementary set of GAAP (refer back to the section of chapter 7 on small business enterprises), the primary difference in accounting for NFPOs is in its recording of contributions to the organization.[2] The organization can choose to follow the restricted-fund method of accounting or the deferral method of accounting.

Overview of Accounting for NFPO Contributions

Contributions to NFPOs are often provided for a specified purpose, such as a building project, a particular service of the organization, or an endowment fund. These are referred to as restricted contributions. These contributions must, therefore, be tracked and reported in a way that ensures that they are used for their specified purpose. One approach is to provide more detail to the reader of the financial statements about each fund and how it is used by setting up a separate fund for each type of specified contribution. Each fund would have its own statement of contributions and expenditures. Alternatively, the NFPO could use an aggregated approach that treats contributions as a liability, likened to deferred revenue. In this approach, the NFPO would recognize contributions only when expenditures related to their specified purpose are recognized. The second (deferral) method provides a more aggregated representation of the funds obtained by an organization. The board will thus have to decide how much detail they wish to disclose about fund activity in the financial statements and ensure it complies with regulations in its jurisdiction.

Benchmarking in NFPOs

Benchmarking is as important for NFPOs as it is for FPOs. The actual benchmarking instruments may be quite different and should reflect the underlying goals of the organization. It is important for the board to not only understand the benchmarking measure of the NFPO but also assess the appropriateness of the measures. Do these measures fit with the mandate of the organization? Is the organization focusing on the right measures?

Often, the benchmarking measures for an NFPO are nonfinancial or are a hybrid of both financial and nonfinancial measures. One common financial measure is the administration costs as a percentage of contributions, that is, how much money is used in running administrative operations versus providing services to benefit the NFPO's cause. Examples of nonfinancial measures are the number of patients serviced in a given year for a hospital or the liters of blood collected in a current year for Canadian Blood Services. An example of a hybrid measure for a hospital is the cost per patient per day.

Disclosure Differences Between NFPOs and FPOs

Central to the annual reports of FPOs are their financial statements and, in particular, the income statement. For an NFPO, these statements may not be of as much importance or prominence within the annual report. Due the differences in focus between these two types of organizations as mentioned previously, the actual financial statements of the NFPO may be viewed as a necessary gate-keeping tool but not as a significant tool in determining the value or performance of the organization.

For example, continuing with a review of the financial statements of the Edmonton Community Foundation, we see immediately the increased amount of detailed disclosure provided in their annual report in comparison to an FPO. The report itself is 69 pages and, yet, the financial statement themselves are only 9 pages in length and are not presented until the 58th page. If location is any indication of importance, then what does this say of the perceived importance of the financial statements to the readers of the report? Likewise, the report of the Auditor General of any country, state, province, or municipality is likely to be several hundred pages long. The presence of legal restrictions on the use of assets and the lack of a profit motive make it difficult to aggregate numbers across different legally constituted fund accounts. This makes the reports very long and detailed. Given this reporting structure, it is even more important that management and the board identify a small set of critical success factors and communicate those factors to the readers of the financial reports.

The Board's Role: Establishing a Strong Mandate

The role of the board in the NFPO is as important, if not more important, than in the FPO. NFPOs are often faced with poor internal control structures and high opportunity for fraudulent activities. As discussed earlier, revenues are more vulnerable to theft. Lack of clear profit criteria means that the NFPO's priorities are expressed via budgets. The board must thus have a more direct role in preparing and approving budgets to ensure that they reflect the mandate of the organization.

NFPO boards are often volunteer boards of individuals who have some connection to the underlying purpose of the organization. These boards can often be comprised of individuals with limited financial or organizational knowledge. These individuals are then charged with the responsibility of ensuring that the organization meets the mandate that it has set for itself, a mandate that may be quite complex and involve constituencies with a very diverse set of interests. Since donors usually have high concerns about overhead (especially fundraising costs) and integrity of the organization, it is important that the underlying internal control and financial reporting systems are operating effectively.

Key Points

1. NFPOs have a distinctly different goal from FPOs. Maximization of shareholder wealth is no longer relevant; instead, the organization is focused on achieving a stated purpose to its greatest ability.
2. The GAAP for NFPOs differs from those for FPOs due to the difference in organizational objectives.
3. The goals of the NFPOs are often defined by the board of directors and budgets are used to operationalize their goals.
4. Benchmarking in the NFPO sector often includes a significant number of nonfinancial measures or hybrid measures, both financial and nonfinancial in nature.
5. Due to the lack of share ownership in an NFPO and the nature of donations, internal control weaknesses may be more prevalent.

Steps for the Board

1. What is the organization's mandate?
   - Ask significant stakeholders about their perception of the purpose and mandate of the organization.
   - Ask management if it believes the actions and programs of the organization match its mandate and purpose.
   - Based on the board's knowledge of the organization and the requests of donors and funding agencies, assess the appropriateness of the mandate.
2. What risks does the organization face? Where do internal control weaknesses exist?
   - Review the organizational chart to determine whether the organization has the appropriate number of staff to allow for segregation of duties.
   - Ensure that the organization's staff has the ability to contact someone other than the executive director/top management should a problem occur.
   - Determine whether the organization has staff who possess the necessary knowledge and experience to function in their duties. Question management as to the training of staff and the level of experience and education of the staff.

3. What measures does the organization use as benchmarks for performance?
   - Question both stakeholders and management to determine whether the benchmarks being utilized meet the mandate of the organization.
   - Based on the mandate and discussion with management, determine what the key drivers for success are for the organization.
   - Determine who the significant stakeholders and clients of the organization are by reviewing the list of significant funding sources and users of the organizations services.
   - Assess whether the benchmarks being used capture the key performance criteria of the organization.
   - Define the board's role in benchmarking. Does the board, an outside party (funding agency), or management set the benchmarks?
4. Is the disclosure in the annual report adequate and appropriate?
   - Ensure all necessary benchmarks are presented.
   - Ensure detailed disclosure is presented for required fund expenditures, such as the number of significant scholarships awarded and to whom.
   - Highlight significant successes of the organization in the annual report.
   - Ensure the continuing needs of the organization and the organization's ability to continue to meet the needs of its beneficiaries are evident.

Conclusion

Accounting is undergoing a transition in financial reporting and interpretation that creates a wide opening for human judgment to enter. Accounting regulators are politically astute and very clever in invoking appealing concepts such as neutrality, transparency, fair value, consistency, and comparability. These concepts, however, must be understood in a very specialized way in accounting settings. Accounting reports provide a highly aggregated accounting representation of the financial condition of an organization. The correspondence between this accounting representation and the underlying economic condition of the firm may or may not be well aligned. An insistence on forcing all organizations to follow the same accounting standards (an attempt to achieve comparability and consistency) increasingly means that standards developed for a small subset of publicly traded, profit-oriented corporations are applied across the economy to private companies, not-for-profit entities, and even governments. For most of these entities, the accounting reports produced are complex, costly, and of questionable benefit for both internal and external decision makers.

The current system of accounting is a hybrid—a legacy of historical cost (stewardship orientation) together with a more recent shift toward a fair value (predicting future cash flow orientation) reporting system. There has been a change in emphasis from reflecting and promoting the interest of creditors and private owners of companies to giving primacy to financial analysts and competitors who want to predict the future cash flows of the firm. This transition is changing the notion and impact of conservatism. Under a historical cost system, conservatism is a desirable attribute of accounting. Under a fair value reporting system, conservatism can be construed as a form of earnings management and trigger regulatory investigations. The accounting system creates a series of distortions, and the amount of distortion is increasing over time. In a perfect world, liquid markets would exist (or be in development) for all assets and liabilities so that fair value accounting (mark-to-market) could be done with little distortion. In the world we live in, this is unlikely to occur in the near future (or ever), and, instead of creating transparency, fair value accounting requires reliance on models that give management tremendous leeway to make assumptions about how future events will occur. The implementation of fair value accounting often leads to wishful thinking and mark-to-myth rather than mark-to-market.

The accounting standard setters are focused on fixing the distortions created by historical cost accounting in the balance sheet. The solution of moving to fair value accounting, however, is undermining the usefulness of the income statement. No one should believe that the financial statements report the "truth" about a company. Instead of educating the public about the complexities and limitations of financial statements, regulators are creating false confidence by having CEOs and CFOs sign certifications. The true economic value of assets and liabilities depends on cash flows that will occur in the future. Since management can forecast the future only approximately and has biased incentives, accounting will always be imprecise and subject to manipulation. Slogans about truth, transparency, and neutrality fail to make accounting more accurate or more useful.

To improve accounting, we recommend two key reforms that a board can ask for internally, even if these reports are not provided to external constituencies. The first reform is to report an explicit breakdown of operating versus investing activity. It is important for the board (and also the investors) to understand how much income is made from operations and to not allow financing to obscure the profitability of operating activity. The U.S. Financial Accounting Standards Board (FASB) is currently considering a proposal to require such a breakdown in all financial statements (i.e., cash flow statement, balance sheet, income statement). A board that wants to be ahead of the regulators can request such a breakdown before the regulators require it.

The second reform is to provide a more forthright depiction of the layers of financial reporting, arranged in order of how objectively (verifiably) each item is measured. This helps to signal the hardness of accounting numbers (or lack thereof) and also makes visible assets (e.g., research and development, community goodwill) and liabilities (e.g., cleanup costs for environmental reclamation) that are currently not reported in the financial statements.

The board and external investors should use financial statements as a starting resource to better understand their specific organization, especially in an environment of transition. They should recognize that financial statements only help one to get started and will not provide a complete understanding of all aspects of an organization. Truth and neutrality in accounting are simply political slogans contributing to mystery rather than meaningful descriptions of accounting practice. To navigate through the challenges and transitions, an effective director will understand accounting's relationship with an organization's risks and opportunities while recognizing that accounting involves human judgment and compromise in both preparing and using financial reports.

APPENDIX 1

Definitions of Some Key Accounting Terms

Page	Term
10	Agency problem (classical definition)
52, 63	Benchmarking
41	Bill and hold
5, 34, 90	Certification
9	Comprehensive income
34	Control culture
33	Control self-assessment (CSA)
84	Deferral method of accounting
76	Differential reporting
47	Earnings before interest, taxes, depreciation, and amortization (EBITDA)
57	Economic value added
8, 9, 12, 13, 47–49, 62, 89, 90	Fair value accounting
6, 61, 64	Generally Accepted Accounting Principles (GAAP)
6	Going concern assumption
71	Harmonization (of GAAP)
8, 13, 29, 46, 48, 61, 90	Historical cost accounting
34, 86	Internal Control System
Appendix 1	International Accounting Standards (IAS)
1, 71–74, 82, 84	International Financial Reporting Standards (IFRS)
59, 90	Mark-to-Market
48, 59, 89	Mark-to-Model
62, 90	Mark-to-Myth
28, 47, 61, 81	Net income
81	Not-for-profit organizations (NFPOs)
42, 44, 45, 59	Off balance sheet

Page	Term
41	Quality of income analysis
11, 40, 64	Reserve
84	Restricted-fund method of accounting
11, 17–22, 37–41, 43, 64, 78, 81–83	Revenue
1, 14, 34, 76–77	Sarbanes-Oxley Act of 2002 (SOX)
75	Small business enterprise (SBE)
53–56	Transaction structuring
1, 5–7, 43–44, 46, 53, 60, 89–90	Transparency

Agency Problem: Occurs when management pursues its own interests that are not in line with those of shareholders. Results from lack of alignment between management and shareholders interests. The manager acts as the agent for the shareholder and the shareholder does not have direct access to the decisions within the entity.

Benchmarking: Key accounting metrics used by the organization's management to run the business and measure its own performance.

Bill and Hold: A method of revenue recognition where the company bills customers for goods without actually sending out the goods to the customer. Revenue is recorded by the entity while the goods are still in its possession and control, which fails to match the economic reality of the transaction.

Certification: The Sarbanes-Oxley Act of 2002 requires the CEO and CFO to certify that the annual and quarterly reports (a) fully comply with the Securities Exchange Act of 1934, (b) the information fairly presents, in all material respects, the company's financial condition and results of operations, and (c) there is compliance with certain provisions of the securities laws.

Comprehensive Income: Change in equity (net assets) of an enterprise during the reporting period from transactions and other events and circumstances from nonowner sources. (International Accounting Standard [IAS] 1 "Presentation of Financial Statements") Includes the income from operations (net income) of the entity and any changes in fair values recorded on the balance sheet. Disclosed below the net income line on the income statement.

Control Culture: "Actions, policies and procedures that reflect the overall attitudes of top management, the directors and the owners of an entity about control and its importance to the entity."[1]

Control Self-Assessment (CSA): Program run by the Institute of Internal Auditors in Canada that seeks to promote good control by empowering frontline employees to understand control objectives. Under CSA, internal auditors become coaches who help workers design better control systems, as opposed to being fraud or error detectors.

Deferral Method of Accounting: Revenue from designated contributions is recognized in the financial statements when the designated expenditures are recognized.

Differential Reporting: Reporting requirements within GAAP that allow for small business enterprises to avoid some of the more complex accounting regulations.

Earnings Before Interest, Taxes, Depreciation, and Amortization (EBITDA): A non-GAAP measure used to report on and evaluate an organization's performance. Commonly thought of as an organization's earnings from operations.

Economic Value Added (EVA): A measure of profit after adjusting for distortions created by accounting. Residual profit after subtracting the company's cost of capital.

Fair Value Accounting: Accounting for assets and liabilities at the value for which they can be realized in the absence of an intention to liquidate. Under fair value accounting, some assets are marked to market, some assets are marked to a model, and some assets are "marked to myth."

Generally Accepted Accounting Principles (GAAP): These are the policies and regulations that govern the recording, preparation, and presentation of financial statements for both public and private organizations. There is currently Canadian GAAP (developed in Toronto), U.S. GAAP (developed in Norwalk) and International GAAP (IAS, developed in London). Canadian companies listed on U.S. stock exchanges can use either Canadian or U.S. GAAP in filings with Canadian regulators. U.S. regulators are currently proposing to allow all foreign registrants (many of whom are Canadian companies) to file their financial statements using either U.S. GAAP or International GAAP.

Going Concern Assumption: Financial statements are prepared based on the assumption that the entity is a going concern. Financial statement users and preparers foresee that the organization will continue normal operations into the future.

Harmonization (of GAAP): Harmonization refers to the movement toward one standard of accounting in a global marketplace. Note there is no move to harmonize legal processes, governance, securities market regulation, or other elements in the financial reporting system.

Historical Cost Accounting: Traditional method of accounting where assets and liabilities are recorded at their original cost less accumulated amortization.

Internal Control System: "Internal controls are the policies and procedures instituted and maintained by the management of an entity in order to (1) maintain reliable control systems, (2) safeguard assets including records, (3) optimize the use of entity resources, and (4) prevent and detect error and fraud."[2]

International Accounting Standards (IAS): Refer to International Financial Reporting Standards.

International Financial Reporting Standards (IFRS): Standards and interpretations issued by the International Accounting Standards Board. Prior to 2001, international standards were issued by the International Accounting Standards Committee (IASC) and labeled International Accounting Standards (IAS). This label has been retained, and standards issued post-2001 are called IFRS. Many nations have adopted IFRS, while others are in the process of converging with these standards.

Mark-to-Market: The act of adjusting the financial statement balance for an item (security, derivative, etc.) to an available market price. A simplified example would be to adjust the carrying value of a marketable security to the price of the security on its applicable exchange at the balance sheet date. For this item, there is a clear market for which a market price can be derived. This practice becomes more prevalent as the accounting standards move toward fair value accounting.

Mark-to-Model: The act of adjusting the financial statement balance for an item (security, derivative, etc.) to a modeled value. In this case, there is no readily available market for the item, so instead a model is derived and utilized to determine a proxy for the market value of the security. A simplified example would be to adjust the carrying value of a derivative to the current value based on a model that takes into account interest rates, stock prices, and/or currency values. Due to the fact that derivative contracts vary in duration and can run for up to 20 years or more, their values are often tied to several values that need to be estimated in order to derive a current market value.

Mark-to-Myth: The tendency for management to be overly optimistic when estimating values used within the model to determine the market value. In the extreme, both parties to a contract might arrive at such different estimates that both are recognizing a gain on this contract through their adjustment to market. In this extreme case, this practice produces a mythical situation as one party to the contract must lose if the other gains on the contract. The term was coined by Warren Buffett of Berkshire Hathaway.

Net Income: The amount of an entity's total sales (revenue) remaining after subtracting all costs (expenses) in a given time period.

Not-for-Profit Organizations (NFPOs): Entities, normally without transferable ownership interests, organized and operated exclusively for social, educational, professional, religious, health, charitable, or any other not-for-profit purposes. They have no direct owners, and the activities of the organization center primarily on the public good.

Off Balance Sheet: The failure to recognize an asset or a liability on the balance sheet of the organization when a right to property (asset) or an obligation (liability) exists. A common example of off-balance-sheet financing is the use of an operating lease to purchase a piece of equipment. By structuring the lease to fall into the criteria of an operating lease, the entity can avoid recognizing the asset and related debt with regards to this equipment on their balance sheet. For a company that is leveraged, the ability to hide this liability may be highly desirable.

Quality of Income Analysis: Also called an earnings quality analysis, it is a comparison of cash flows to reported income to reveal the level of accounting accruals used by management.

$$\text{Quality of Income} = \text{Operating Cash Flow} \div \text{Net Income}$$

Reserve: Income that management has deferred in order to allow future recognition of this income. In the context of earnings management, a reserve represents income held until some future period when it may be advantageous to recognize it. Reserves can be set up by increasing the allowance for doubtful accounts, deferral of revenue recognition, and so on.

Restricted-Fund Method of Accounting: The organization sets up a separate fund for each type of designated contribution. All receipts and expenditures related to a specific fund are recorded as activities of that fund.

Revenue: An increase in economic resources, either by way of inflows or enhancements of assets or reductions of liabilities, resulting from the ordinary activities of an entity (e.g., sales, rent, or donations). It is important to note that revenue is calculated prior to the deduction of the entity's expenses.

Sarbanes-Oxley Act of 2002 (SOX): A U.S. legislation enacted in 2002 in response to the high-profile financial statement scandals of Enron and World-Com. SOX is administered by the Securities and Exchange Commission and covers issues such as auditor independence, corporate governance, internal control assessment, and enhanced financial disclosure.

Small Business Enterprises (SBE): Enterprises that have a small number of financial statement users. Excludes public enterprises, cooperative organizations, pension plans, or financial institutions.

Transaction Structuring: The act of structuring a transaction to meet a specific goal of management. In an accounting context, transaction structuring refers to structuring the actual contractual elements of the contract to obtain a specific accounting treatment for an item. An example of transaction structuring would be to include conditions within a lease contract so that the lease can be classified as an operating lease as opposed to a capital lease that would require the recognition of an asset and liability on the organization's financial statements.

Transparency: In the context of financial reporting, transparency refers to the degree of detail provided in the financial statements (including note disclosure).

APPENDIX 2

Further Reading

Chapter 1

Mismatching Audit Firms With the Organization: Friehling and Horowitz (Madoff Auditors)

Securities and Exchange Commission v. David G. Friehling, C.P.A. and Friehling & Horowitz, CPAs, P.C. (S.D.N.Y. Civ. 09 CV 2467). Retrieved August 16, 2009, from http://www.sec.gov/litigation/litreleases/2009/lr20959.htm

Chapter 3

Safeway Annual Report 2008

Safeway Inc. (2008). 2008 Annual Report. Retrieved June 10, 2009, from http://www.sec.gov/

Nortel Restatements, Revenue Recognition Issues, and Accounting Complexity

Taub, S. (2007, March 1). Nortel adds another "re" to restatement. www.CFO.com. Retrieved August 16, 2009, from http://www.cfo.com/article.cfm/8792226/c_8771072

Parmalat Accounting Fraud Involving Cash

The Motley Fool. (2009, July 27). Famous scams: Parmalat. www.fool.co.uk. Retrieved August 16, 2009, from http://www.fool.co.uk/news/investing/2009/07/27/famous-scams-parmalat.aspx

Chapter 5

Deloitte Survey on Issues Important to Corporate Directors

Deloitte Touche Tomatsu. (2007). In the dark II: What many boards and executives STILL don't know about the health of their business. Retrieved May 18, 2009, from http://www.deloitte.com/assets/Dcom-Global/Local%20Assets/Documents/dtt_Audit_IntheDark033007.pdf

Wal-Mart Transaction Structuring Regarding Income Taxes

Drucker, J. (2007, February 1). Friendly landlord: Wal-Mart cuts taxes by paying rent to itself; other retailers, banks use loophole in rules to lower states' levies. *Wall Street Journal* (Eastern Edition), p. A1. Retrieved August 16, 2009, from ProQuest ABI/INFORM Global database.

Microsoft in Ireland

Simpson, G. R. (2005, November 7). Wearing of the green: Irish subsidiary lets Microsoft slash taxes in U.S. and Europe; tech and drug firms move key intellectual property to low-levy island haven; center of windows licensing. *Wall Street Journal* (Eastern Edition), p. A1. Retrieved August 16, 2009, from ProQuest ABI/INFORM Global database.

Earnings Management by Manipulating Real Accounting Transactions

Graham, J. R., Harvey, C. R., & Rajgopal, S. (2005). The economic implications of corporate financial reporting. *Journal of Accounting & Economics*, 40(1–3), 3–73. Retrieved August 16, 2009, from Proquest ABI/INFORM Global database.

Options Backdating Scandal

Forelle, C., & Bandler, J. (2006, March 18). The perfect payday; some CEOs reap millions by landing stock options when they are most valuable; luck—or something else? *Wall Street Journal* (Eastern Edition), p. A1. Retrieved August 17, 2009, from ProQuest ABI/INFORM Global database.

Costco Wholesale Corporation 2008 Annual Report

Costco Wholesale Corporation. (2009). *2008 Annual Report.* Retrieved June 10, 2009, from http://www.sec.gov

Loblaws 2008 Annual Report

Loblaw Companies Limited. (2009). *2008 Annual Report.* Retrieved June 10, 2009, from http://sedar.com/

Chapter 6

Too Much Disclosure: AT&T and MCI-WorldCom

Martin, D. (2004). *Tough calls: AT&T and the hard lessons learned from the Telecom wars.* New York: AMACOM.

Mark-to-Myth: A Term Coined by Warren Buffett in Reference to Derivatives

Weinberg, A. (2003, May 9). The great derivatives smackdown. www.forbes.com. Retrieved August 16, 2009, from http://www.forbes.com/2003/05/09/cx_aw_0509derivatives.html

Appendix 1

Definitions of Some Key Accounting Terms

Arens, A. A., Elder, R. J., Beasley, M. S., & Splettstoesser-Hogeterp, I. B. (2007). *Auditing and other assurance services* (Canadian 10th ed.). Toronto: Pearson Prentice Hall.

Notes

Introduction

1. The Safeway Inc. 2008 Annual Report can be downloaded from the U.S. Securities and Exchange Commission at http://www.sec.gov/Archives/edgar/vprr/09/9999999997-09-017436

Chapter 1

1. R&D expenditures clearly create an economic asset for a company. However, accounting rules consider R&D an expense, thus penalizing managers who make good operating decisions.

2. An alternative argument is that conservative accounting standards help counter management's bias to report aggressively, thus resulting in neutral accounting numbers. However, accounting standard setters explicitly reject the adoption of conservative standards and insist that standards should be neutral. If they succeed in achieving neutrality in standards, then the resulting accounting numbers are likely to be biased.

3. Research evidence suggests that investors like (and reward) companies who report a smooth pattern of earnings.

4. The use of a statement of comprehensive income, which separately presents unrealized losses and gains, attempts to prevent these items from being lumped together with real cash flows, but the additional disclosure and ambiguous label might contribute to confusion for some financial statement users.

5. The board should understand how good their auditor is. If you have a bad auditor, you will have poor reporting and/or lengthy, unproductive arguments over accounting issues. A good auditor will have a clear stance on accounting issues but will be open to productive debate with the board and management.

6. *Securities and Exchange Commission v. David G. Friehling, C.P.A. and Friehling & Horowitz, CPAs, P.C. (2009).*

Chapter 3

1. Taub (2007).
2. The Motley Fool (2009).
3. Safeway Inc. (2008) Annual Report, Form 10-K, p. 23.
4. Again, care must be taken not to be too conservative in financial reporting. Excessive conservatism can be construed to be fraudulent reporting, since it is a departure from neutral reporting.

Chapter 4

1. Safeway Inc. (2008) Annual Report, Form 10-K, p. 40.

2. XBRL is a coding language that preparers use to organize and communicate electronic financial information. Users then read and analyze financial information electronically using XBRL software.

3. Safeway Inc. (2008) Annual Report, Form 10-K, p. 54.

4. Safeway Inc. (2008) Annual Report, Form 10-K, p. 41.

5. Safeway Inc. (2008) Annual Report, Form 10-K, p. 8.

6. Safeway Inc. (2008) Annual Report, Form 10-K, p. 42.

7. Safeway Inc. (2008) Annual Report, Form 10-K, p. 30.

Chapter 5

1. Deloitte Touche Tomatsu (2007).

2. Loblaw Companies Limited (2009).

3. Costco Wholesale Corporation (2009).

4. Drucker (2007).

5. It has also attracted some publicity for setting up a holding company in Ireland that owns all of Microsoft's intellectual property (Simpson, 2005). All Microsoft company operations (including those in the United States) pay a royalty to the Irish holding company as a royalty fee, which is estimated to be about $500 million annually. Despite attention from the financial press, there doesn't appear to be any tax audits conducted of Microsoft's intellectual capital management practices. According to the Simpson article, several drug companies are also engaged in similar practices, leading to tax leakage from the United States and all countries around the world in which these companies operate.

6. Graham, Harvey, and Rajgopal (2005).

7. Forelle and Bandler (2006).

Chapter 6

1. Many companies use nonaccounting numbers in their external reporting (e.g., the widespread use of Earnings Before Interest, Taxes, Depreciation and Amortization [EBITDA]) and in their executive compensation contracts a (e.g., Nortel's use of pro forma earnings to calculate management bonuses). While regulators often view such numbers with suspicion (and insist that they be reconciled with GAAP numbers), a good case can be made that these measures are value relevant because of deficiencies in computation of GAAP numbers.

2. It has been suggested that AT&T spent an enormous amount of time dissecting the financial statements of MCI-WorldCom (Martin, 2004). Michael

Armstrong's strategy for AT&T was derailed by the misconceptions due to extensive study of MCI-WorldCom's (fraudulent) financial statements.

3. A Ponzi scheme is a type of fraud where investments by new shareholders are reported as operating income to current shareholders to inflate the apparent profitability of the company. A big concern about income trusts was that, while cash flows were being reported and distributed, there was a lack of proper accounting and reporting standards to ascertain whether cash distributions were coming from operating income, a return of capital, or a combination of both.

4. Weinberg (2003).

5. Measuring *quality* and *amount* of disclosure is challenging since these concepts are so abstract. Researchers have not reached a consensus as to what constitutes good quality disclosure. An example of such a debate is whether more frequent disclosure reflects a higher quality of disclosure.

Chapter 7

1. Source: The CICA's Guide to IFRS in Canada.

2. IFRS has a similar framework to that of Canadian and U.S. GAAP, but there are differences in the detailed application and standards in some areas. Due to the differences in standards, there may be process changes to the financial statements. A detailed list of these differences is outside of the goal of this book, but the board must be aware that differences in the accounting treatment and reporting of some items may be caused by the conversion.

Chapter 8

1. There is a misguided attempt underway to force all NFPO and even government agencies to use the same accounting standards (GAAP) as those developed for FPOs. A university can be forced to compute costs such as depreciation, though it is not clear if computing such accounting numbers serves any purpose or if it is of any value to users of financial statements.

2. NFPO-specific announcements are found in CICA Handbook Section 4400 in Canada and FASB 116 and 117 in the United States.

Appendix A

1. Arens, Elder, Beasley, and Splettstoesser-Hogeterp (2007), p. 247.

2. Arens et al. (2007), p. 243.

Index

Note: The *italicized f* following page numbers refers to figures.